Canvas Décor

*25+ No-Sew, Low-Sew
Projects for Your Home*

Bunny DeLorie

©2004 Bunny DeLorie
Published by

kp books
An imprint of F+W Publications, Inc.

700 East State Street • Iola, WI 54990-0001
715-445-2214 • 888-457-2873

The following registered trademark terms and companies appear in this publication:
Aleene's® Platinum Bond™ Super Fabric Textile Adhesive, Converse® All Star®, Crafter's
Pick™, Dacron®, DecoArt™ Americana® Acrylic Paint, DecoArt™ Brush 'n Blend™,
DecoArt™ Faux Glazing Medium™, DecoArt™ No-Prep™ Metal Paint, DecoArt™ Patio
Paint™, Delta Ceramcoat®, Keds®, Krylon®, Minwax®, Mylar®, Plaid® FolkArt®,
Prismacolor®, Stensource®, Styrofoam™, Tight 'n' Up™, Transfer Tool™, Tulip® Cool Color
Spray™, Tulip® Rub-On Transfers™, Tulip® Soft™ Brushable Fabric Paint and Yasutomo
Fabric Mate™.

Library of Congress Catalog Number: 2004105221

ISBN: 0-87349-848-8

Edited by Sarah Herman
Designed by Sharon Laufenberg

Printed in the United States of America

Acknowledgments

This book is a result of the tireless effort and dedication of so many special people whose enthusiasm and talent made it all possible. I am deeply grateful to all of them for their continued support and would like to acknowledge the following:

David DeLorie, my husband, who is the biggest supporter of my dreams and goals. He encourages me in all of my crazy and wild ideas, no matter what they are, because he believes that if I believe in them, then I'll find a way to make them happen. David is also able to figure out how to make something that I'm envisioning in my head. Anyone who can spend hours rebuilding a 100-year-old watch must have a lot of patience. We balance each other perfectly.

Janet Newell, the contributing writer, who became a long-time friend the first day I met her. Her talents include not only writing, editing and Web site design, but also home decorating and sewing. As a team, Janet and I put our heads together to come up with loads of ideas in just an afternoon.

Craig Cook, photographer, who I've worked with since "Aleene's Creative Living." Even though he doesn't understand how a craft or decorating project is made, he takes the photo as if he understands every single step.

Kim Kapellusch, senior photo stylist, who has the amazing knack of visualizing an entire room. Whether it's setting up a single object for photography or an entire vignette, Kim has an extraordinary eye.

Julie Stephani, book acquisitions editor for KP Books, who believed in the "Canvas Décor" book concept from the first morning I mentioned it to her. Always smiling and eager to listen, Julie makes you feel like your idea is the best one since sliced bread.

Sarah Herman, editor for KP Books, whose expertise kept me on track and on time.

Cody Montano and Monica DeBolt, the "model" children, whose animated style helped achieve a very natural look. Monica is the granddaughter of my long-time high school friend, Vicky. Cody is my grandson from our daughter, Paula. I do believe that both of the children are animated because they are chips off the family trees!

Chantal Guy, hand model, who sat patiently for hours during photo shoots. She is a lovely lady and a talented designer with her own handmade scarves, hats, purses and more. By the time we finished the photo shoots, Chantal was also into home decorating with canvas!

My long-time friends at Wall Lenk Corporation for their support and for providing my favorite tools.

My friends at Duncan Enterprises who have always given me the best help and incredible products.

Donna and Jerry from Canvas Concepts who introduced me to a whole new line of fabulous canvas craft materials.

Table of Contents

Introduction

When I think back to what might have been my first "crafting project," I remember making dresses for my Barbie doll. Now, we're not talking about sewing, we're talking about gluing! Yes, I would make them from felt because the cut edges didn't fray and my little round-nosed scissors would cut the felt. Do you remember those scissors?

Oh, I had fashions no one had ever seen! Using thin cardboard from cake boxes, I made a variety of fashionable brimmed hats covered with felt and "jewels" like sequins, beads and trims for the perfect accessory. Of course, then I needed the purse to go with the stunning ensemble! I drew the line at shoes. I tried it, but came to the conclusion I was not a cobbler.

I must have been seven or eight years old, but I remember my grandmother saying to me one day as she admired my designer outfits, "Some day you are going to be a designer!" Of course I thought, "I'm just playing and I don't even know what a designer really is, but okay."

So here I am today ... faux finisher, decorative painter, TV host, instructor and, yes, designer. I guess you could say I wear a lot of hats! And, by the way, you should see my closet now ... I must own 50 hats! I love hats!

My most recent exploration has been my work with canvas fabric. It's versatile. It's affordable. And it's the hot new material for home décor.

That's right. Canvas isn't just for floorcloths anymore. In this book, you'll find a wide variety of home décor projects for the do-it-yourselfer that add charm to each room in the house. I've included projects using a number of techniques like sewing, stenciling, faux painting and embellishment with other materials. Unexpected projects in each chapter, such as the Tomato Cage Garden Accent Light, will surprise and delight even the most experienced crafter.

My projects are presented by chapter in popular themes. A photo vignette of the themed projects will show them in a completed setting. Projects range from easy to more involved, but never difficult. Techniques are explained in detail with step-by-step instructions accompanied by dozens of color photos.

I hope to inspire you to get excited about the unique and creative projects using this easy-to-find "blank canvas."

Chapter ①

Canvas Basics

Origins of Canvas

When people hear the word "canvas," most of them probably think of the starchy white fabric stretched over a wooden frame—the surface of choice used by just about every known (and unknown) artist to paint their works of art on for the last five hundred years.

However, "canvas" is also a term used to describe a tightly woven fabric. Today, canvas is usually made of cotton or linen, but that hasn't always been the case.

The word "canvas" is derived from the word "cannabis," the Latin word for hemp. For centuries, hemp was widely used as a textile fiber. When American cotton began to overtake the market in the beginning of the nineteenth century, hemp production went into a tailspin. The name "canvas" remained the same.

In the beginning ...

Believe it or not, canvas has actually been around—in one form or another—for thousands of years. Thanks to its strength and versatility, this wonderful fabric played a major role in the spread of human civilization and helped shape the world!

Flax fibers are among the oldest and strongest known to man. The oldest woven cloth on record is linen. In fact, evidence for the use of natural flax fibers has been found in Stone Age dwellings.

But since flax has been cultivated for eons and in so many different countries, its exact origins are obscure. While some believe flax was first cultivated in the Nile Delta ten thousand years ago, others believe it can be traced to the Caucasus, between the Persian Gulf and the Caspian and Black Seas.

Okay, so the actual "birthplace" may be unknown, but, when it comes to common flax (linum usitatissimum), it certainly lives up to its name! Translated from Latin, usitatissimum means "most useful."

It's a wrap!

The Ancient Egyptians were very familiar with flax, and it was held in the highest regard. When the process of mummification was first developed around 3,000 B.C., the early embalmers used linen of flax fibers to ceremoniously wrap the dead. The linen, which was usually provided by the family of the deceased, was soaked in sacramental herbs, oils and ointments. Flax plants also decorated the tombs. Yet, because of the high quality of the fabric, coupled with the dry Egyptian climate, mummified linen has survived for over 6,000 years!

While an obvious favorite with the Pharoahs to produce linen, annual and perennial flax was also used (and still is today) to make rope, string, measuring line, bags, purses, thread, fish nets, bed sheets and the all-important sail.

By land and by sea ...

As a wonderful material to make sails for sea-faring ships, flax/linen can be considered a major contributor for the spread of culture throughout the world as the early mariners made their way from ancient Egypt to Phoenicia, Mesopotamia, Greece and Rome.

But it wasn't only the ancient sailors who understood the benefits of flax/linen for sails. Its use for sailing larger vessels was especially important to the world's greatest explorers. The renowned Mayflower, along with many other ships throughout history, had sails made from the plant's fibers.

It basically wasn't until the early 1950s that the standard canvas sailcloth, which over time had a tendency to rot, was replaced with Dacron. Today, a wide variety of manmade fibers are used in sailing, but they are all based on the same basic design.

Canvas was just as essential to surviving land exploration as it was to surviving the sea. The most common covered wagons used by the early settlers were the conestoga and the prairie schooner. While the conestogas were pulled by teams of six or eight horses and could haul up to five tons, the prairie schooner was smaller and sleeker. The "bonnets" used for both wagons was usually a homespun cotton canvas doubled over to make them watertight.

Pack it up!

And while canvas was also used for tents and protection from the elements, it was a poor French-Canadian named Camille Poirer who first filed for a patent for a "packsack" in 1882, just ten years after moving to Duluth. It was a canvas sack that closed with a buckled flap, had new-fangled shoulder straps in addition to the traditional tumpline, a revolutionary sternum strap and an umbrella holder (for portable shade in this newly cut-over country). Known then as the Poirer Pack, this northwoods classic is referred to today as the original Duluth Pack.

Camille sold off the pack business in 1911 to the Duluth Tent and Awning Company, which boasts a booming business today. Not surprising, their early catalogs feature hay wagon covers, cots, wall tents and heavy canvas aprons for working blacksmiths.

Stretching the truth

Artists first turned to using canvas as a painting surface in Italy during the Renaissance. Until then, Medieval paintings where primarily painted on wood surfaces. The blemish-free wood panels were made of well-seasoned wood and often prepared with layers of white linen strips that had been soaked in gesso, a hot water-soluble glue.

Italian artists soon fell in love with the practicalities of painting on fabric rather than wood, as it facilitated storage, shipping and handling. Northern European artists in Belgium, Holland and Germany took longer to convert to "modern ways," and for at least another hundred years continued to paint on wooden panels. But ,as a number of artists flocked to Italy to study, painting on canvas became increasingly widespread.

Cotton canvas was less expensive to purchase than both linen and hemp, but it was not as suitable as a painting surface. Cotton fibers were weaker and more prone to developing mildews and molds. It is only in the last century that cotton has begun to outsell linen for artists' canvas.

The French Impressionists initially used either linen or hemp canvas as a painting medium, but, as hemp became gradually more rare, they relied almost exclusively on linen.

Sneaking around

Before the late 1970s, running shoes were not so high-tech. Until the middle of the nineteenth century, most athletic shoes were made on a single straight canvas and there was no difference between the right or left shoe.

The earliest reference to "sneaks" appears in James Greenwood's account of 1873 London life: "sneaks ... are shoes with canvas tops and India-rubber soles." For nearly one hundred years, this simple description would continue to be an accurate definition of sneakers.

In the United States, Keds were first mass-marketed as canvas-top "sneakers" in 1917 by the U.S. Rubber Company. When choosing a name, the initial favorite was Peds, from the Latin meaning "foot," but the trademark was held by someone else.

The credit for the word "sneaker" actually goes to Henry Nelson McKinney, an advertising agent for N. W. Ayer & Son, because the rubber sole made the shoe stealthy or quiet. At the time, all other shoes, with the exception of moccasins, made noise when people walked.

At the same time, the Converse Rubber Corporation came out with their first version of the All Star basketball shoe in 1917 as well. The All Star came in only one color: black. It consisted of a very thick rubber sole and ankle coverings made of canvas.

Etc., etc., etc.

The wide variety and the versatile use of canvas today are as limitless as your imagination: from top-of-the-line designer handbags and luggage to durable and affordable backpacks and bags; from the expensive linen canvases used by artists to the inexpensive drop-cloths used by house painters; from man's earliest exploration of the world to his exploration beyond.

Types of Canvas

From fabric by-the-yard to framed blanks for artists, canvas comes in many different shapes and sizes. Here are some of the choices:

Unprimed canvas

Most unprimed canvas is fabric that is used for sewing projects. It has no sealer, gesso or finish applied to it. Canvas by-the-yard comes in either 45" or 54" widths and can be purchased at retail fabric stores. Choose a high-quality, closely woven, unprimed canvas for sewing projects such as the director's chairs or canopy panels. Sailmakers sell unprimed canvas in larger sizes. Check out marine, awning or tent suppliers as well.

Wherever you purchase canvas, ask the store clerk to roll the canvas onto a cardboard tube (the kind that is used for wide decorator fabrics) for transporting to avoid wrinkles and creases. Always roll finished canvas floorcloths, tapestries or other panels of canvas on a tube to store.

Do not attempt to wash canvas fabric. It will soften and shrink and become very wrinkled. The wrinkles are extremely difficult to remove. As a matter of fact, only a commercial dry cleaner can professionally steam and roll wrinkled canvas fabric.

Cotton canvas does not have a "wrong" or "right" side. Simply choose the side that has the smoother texture for the front.

The best way to cut canvas is either with a scissors or a rotary cutter with a protective mat underneath. The edges of unprimed canvas will fray if not stitched or sealed with fabric glue.

Primed canvas

Primed canvas is a heavy woven fabric made of flax or cotton. Its surface is typically prepared for painting by priming it with a surfacing material called a ground. Most primed canvas is finished with gesso. The standard canvas is linen, made of flax, and is very strong and long-lasting. A less expensive alternative to linen is heavy cotton duck. Cotton is somewhat less durable than linen because it is more prone to absorb dampness, but is still an acceptable material for fine art.

If you are going to prime and paint canvas fabric, the recommended floorcloth canvas in this book is number 10. It is more readily available and easily sewn. Number 10 is approximately 15 ounces per yard and is available from 52" to 120" widths.

Primed canvas is used for projects that are going to be painted, such as the Vegetable and Fruit Canvas Wall Plaques (see page 68) and the Faux Tile Niche (see page 71).

Double primed canvas

Double primed canvas is canvas that has one coating of gesso on one side (used for the back) and two coats of gesso on the other side (used for the top, or painting side.) By purchasing canvas that is already primed, you'll save time and finish your project more quickly.

Framed canvas

Framed canvas is typically primed canvas stapled tightly onto wood stretcher bars in a variety of sizes used by artists and painters. I've used framed canvas panels in the Tri-Fold Screen with Faux Bamboo Legs (see page 24). If you are unable to find framed canvas in the correct size for your project, refer to the instructions in Chapter 2 for how to make your own framed canvas panels (see page 19).

Drop cloths

Drop cloths are large, relatively low quality canvas pieces that are used mainly to protect floors and furniture from splatters when painting a room. Professional painters prefer canvas drop cloths because, in addition to protecting the surface, they absorb splatters.

Canvas drop cloths are made from recycled mill pound fabrics, generally seconds or thirds that are discarded for various reasons by clothing manufacturers. To tell if you've chosen a good quality canvas drop cloth, check the weave and weight of the product. Experts agree that the heavier the weight and tighter the cotton weave, the better and more absorbent the product.

If you like, you could try using drop cloths for some of the projects, such as the Tomato Cage Garden Accent Light (see page 88), but remember to prime the drop cloth first with gesso.

Tip

If you are worried about the longevity of your paintings or if you paint heavy impasto, you should use a medium to heavy linen. The reason is that cotton has a very short, weak fiber and, therefore, when woven into thread and then into canvas, it is not as strong as linen, which has a longer, stronger fiber and holds together much better over an extended period of time.

The artist's choice

Linen, although expensive, is traditionally the painter's preferred fabric. There are four reasons for this. First, linen is the most durable of all fabrics for painting. The warp and weft threads are equal in weight, making linen less susceptible to expansion and contraction problems from moisture. Second, linen retains its natural oils over time, which preserves fiber flexibility and decreases embrittlement with age. Third, linen is very receptive to sizing and priming films. And, finally, linen is characterized by a uniform surface. It is available in a variety of textures, from smooth to rough, and in weights from light to heavy. Linen maintains its distinctive weave even through layers of paint.

Tools

There are a number of tools to have handy while working on some of the canvas projects. Some are traditional crafting and sewing supplies, while others might seem a bit more unusual.

Acrylic paint: Acrylic or craft paints are readily available in craft stores and come in a multitude of colors.

Artist brush: This is a flat, round or thin line brush used with paint to add decorative details.

Canvas gel: When mixed with acrylic paints for canvas painting, it gives a dimensional look by enabling layering of paint on canvas.

Chip brushes: These are short-bristled, inexpensive brushes made from undyed hog bristles 3" to 4" wide. They are used for texturizing, but not for fine, precise work.

An assortment of tools and supplies needed for making canvas projects.

Electric stencil cutting pen: This pencil-handled, heated tool is similar to a wood-burner and is used to melt Mylar to cut your own stencils.

Fabric marker pens: Watercolor based pens dispense a variety of colors using either a felt or brush tip. They are used to accent images or draw designs and write words or numbers with precision. They will not run when a sealer is applied over them.

Fabric paints: A mixture of acrylic paint and fabric medium, these paints are designed for painting on fabric.

Faux glazing medium: This milky painting substance, when mixed with acrylic paint, increases the flow of the paint to allow more time to work with the paint. It also creates a more translucent look when applied to the surface.

Foam brush and mini foam roller: This absorbent sponge material, mounted on a stick or roller, is used with paint for background and base coat painting. They come in sizes ranging from ½" to 3" wide.

Gesso: This compound is specifically formulated for use on canvas panels to prepare and seal the canvas for painting. Gesso must be diluted 3 to 1 with water and applied with a foam roller, foam brush or 2" nylon brush. The water-based Gesso shrinks the canvas slightly, which tightens it up as it dries.

Glues: The most common adhesives used on canvas are fabric glue, white glue and hot glue. All will bond the fabric together successfully.

Heat transfer tool: This pencil-handled, heated tool transfers black-and-white or color photocopies onto unfinished wood, canvas and primed canvas, cotton blends and some unfinished leathers.

Joint compound: This is a substance used by drywall contractors to cover the nylon tape placed at the joints of drywall sheets. It is available in tubes or plastic tubs. When applied over a stencil, it adds dimension to a project.

Latex paint: Interior latex household paint is water-based and comes in flat, low sheen, eggshell and velvet finishes. It is used for base-coating canvas.

Mylar: This refers to the brand name of clear polyester film that comes in thicknesses of 7ml to 10ml thick and is used in this book for cutting custom stencils.

Natural sea sponge: From nature, these are used to apply paint. They are texturizing tools to add interest to surfaces.

Painter's blue tape: This is a special low tack, adhesive-backed tape used by professional painters to mask off areas not to be painted. The tape comes in widths of ½" to 2".

Palette: This is a container or surface for artists to mix and blend paints. Common containers include aluminum pie plates, paper or plastic plates, foam food trays or genuine artist board palettes.

Photocopies: These are images copied by a photocopy machine. Inkjet printouts will not work with the techniques in these projects.

Pre-cut stencils: The pre-cut stencils used in the book are the patio, stepping stone, reptile and insect stencils.

Primers: Exterior or interior flat latex paint can be used as a substitute for gesso to prime canvas fabric and make it ready for painting techniques. Two or more coats are required.

Red liner tape: This double-sided, very strong tape is available in rolls in a variety of widths from ⅛" to 1¼". It is also available in shapes (stars, circles, etc.).

Spray shellac: A natural resin secreted by the lac bug is used primarily in wood finishes. It can be used for sealing painted or unpainted surfaces.

Stretcher bars: These are wood strips that come in various lengths and fit together to form a frame, either square or rectangular. Canvas is pulled over these stretcher bars to make panels for painting.

Stencil brush: This short, round, stiff-bristled brush is designed for stenciling. It distributes paint evenly in the openings of stencils. It can be single or double ended.

T-square: A ruler with a crosspiece makes perfectly square panel corners.

Transfer paper: This paper has a color coating on one side designed to be positioned between the fabric and a pattern to transfer the design to the fabric by drawing over the design. It comes in a variety of colors.

Water-based sealer: This comes in clear acrylic varnish or polyurethane, and matte, satin and lo-sheen finishes. Sealer comes in a spray, wipe-on or brush variety.

Wood stains: These oil-based wood stains come in a variety of colors and, while they're intended for use on wood, when applied over paint, they create an antique or faux leather look.

An assortment of paints and brushes including outdoor paint, acrylic paint, primers and sealers.

Techniques

Painting and faux finishing has been around for years, and many of the techniques for application to walls can also be used on canvas fabric. Here are some of the fundamental techniques used in our projects.

Glazing

Glazes are created when a glazing medium is mixed with a paint to increase the flow and create a more translucent look. The more glaze added to the paint, the more translucent the paint will look on the surface. The less glaze added to the paint, the more opaque the paint will look. Glazes will not dry out quickly, so there's more time to work with the product.

Washes of color

Washes of color are created with acrylic or latex paint thinned with water. Washes, as with glazes, can vary in opacity. Because the paint is thinned with water, the wash will dry quickly.

Glazes and washes can be dragged, rag-rolled, sponged, stippled, spattered or worked in a stria method.

Stenciling

Stenciling refers to applying color to a stencil using a stenciling brush. The colors are applied in different degrees of lightness and darkness to the open areas of the stencil, called "windows."

Sponging

The simplest of the faux finishing techniques, sponging is created by using a natural sea sponge and either applying paint or a glaze to the surface with a "positive" technique (adding paint over the top of a previous color) or a "negative" technique (removing paint from areas).

Ragging

This effect is achieved by dabbing a "tool" into a wet medium. In this book, you will see that ragging is done with a plastic bag or plastic wrap to distress oil stains.

Dragging or Stria

The stria technique is achieved by applying a glaze to a surface using a brush, then dragging or pulling a foam brush or soft bristle brush through the wet glaze. Let the brush do the work and wipe off any extra glaze from the brush as needed.

Parchment

This technique is achieved with 3" or 4" chip brushes. The tip of the chip brush is dipped into the paint and lightly dry brushed off onto paper towels. The paint is applied to the surface in a criss-cross fashion. The brush is reloaded with paint as needed.

Dry brush

Dry brushing refers to the technique of off-loading paint from a brush onto paper towels, leaving the brush almost free of paint. It is used for highlighting and shading. When the brush is applied to the surface, the paint will not be blotchy.

Antiquing

This is the method of assigning age to an object by applying a stain or glaze medium into cracks and crevices, then removing the excess with a soft cloth. The key to successful antiquing is creating a subtle, uneven appearance. Colors usually used in antiquing are earth tones: raw umber, burnt umber, raw sienna, burnt sienna and black.

Tight 'n' Up

It's the simple things in life that can be so exciting! Just like when I first found this product at a convention. It's the answer to all loose canvas dilemmas and it works!

Too much humidity adds tension to canvas. The lack of humidity does the opposite, loosening canvas. Tight 'n' Up solves both of these problems by first adding humidity, causing the canvas to shrink, and then the wonderful binder agents in the product lock them in place giving the needed support to keep the canvas tension.

How to use:

1 Notice the dent in the palm tree panel.

2 Spray a moderate amount on the back of a painted or unpainted stretched canvas.

3 Tight 'n' Up will not harm the canvas, artist paints or other mediums used to prime the canvas. It is acid-free and archival art material. For complete details, check the label on the bottle.

Chapter  2

Canvas How-To's

Heat Transfer
Tool Instructions

Years ago I was a regular guest/craft demonstrator on "Aleene's Creative Living" show. I was an avid crafter always on the lookout for *new* and *unusual* products to take onto Aleene's program and show the viewers. When I was looking for an electric stencil cutting pen, I called Bob Paul, vice president of Wall Lenk Corporation in North Carolina. Bob and I became good friends and he sent me a prototype of a new heat tool that was being developed for the craft industry. With a piece of wallpaper, a scrap of 2 x 4 wood and the heat tool, the Transfer Tool was born. Bob named it the "Bunny Burner" after me and the rest is crafting history.

Materials

- Heat transfer tool with round head and wire stand*
- Lightweight canvas fabric (unprimed)
- Black-and-white or color laser copies of images (take patterns, drawings, photographs, wrapping paper, wallpaper, gift cards, etc., to an office supply store or print shop and have them copied)

Notes: Ink jet copies printed from a computer printer will not work. Also, please note any copyright restrictions on items you are copying.
* Used in this example: Transfer Tool by Wall Lenk

1 Iron out any wrinkles in the canvas fabric.

2 Attach the round transfer tip to the tool. Lay the tool on the wire resting stand. Plug it in and allow it to heat for at least five minutes.

3 Cut loosely around the copied designs. Place the copies face-down onto the right side of the canvas. Rub the back of the copy slowly with the tool using a circular motion to transfer the images onto the canvas.

4 Transfer one area at a time. Lift up the paper as you transfer to check the progress. If the paper sticks, go over the area lightly to reheat and lift up paper again. The transferred design will have the appearance of an old, worn painting.

5 Unplug the tool and let it cool. Unscrew the tip.

Tips
- Brighter colors transfer better. Have the photocopied image made a notch or two darker than regular copies.
- Use textile paint or textile medium mixed with acrylic paint to embellish the design on the fabric. Mix the textile medium 80/20 percent with acrylic paint. To tint the fabric, dip the fabric into the mixture. Wring out the fabric and either dry flat or line dry.
- Allow 72 hours before washing the fabrics. Heat set the project in a low temperature dryer or with an iron. Hand washing the fabric project is recommended.

Transferring with **Transfer Paper**

Materials
- Unprimed or primed canvas
- Transfer paper—any darker color
- Pencil or pen
- Pattern

1 Place transfer paper, color side down, on the right side of primed or unprimed canvas. Be sure the canvas is placed on a hard surface.

2 Place the design or pattern on top of the transfer paper. Tape it in place, if necessary, to stabilize the pattern and prevent it from moving.

3 Trace around the pattern with a pencil or pen, using steady pressure.

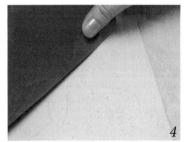

4 Check occasionally by lifting up the pattern to be sure the design is transferring.

Stencil Cutting **Instructions**

I've been designing and hand cutting stencils for years. The first few years I hand-cut the stencils with a craft knife … a very time-consuming task. It also limited the types of designs that I could cut. Delicate designs were out of the question, and it was really hard on the hands! The day I was introduced to the Electric Stencil Cutting Pen by Wall Lenk was the day stencil cutting became a *dream come true*. The stencil patterns in this book can be cut easily with a stencil cutting pen. It's like tracing, but with a hot tip that just melts away the Mylar. I enjoy creating fantastic projects, and anything I can do to save time is a bonus.

Designer **Secrets**

You can find Mylar at art supply stores in larger sizes. Even though both sides can be used for applying paint, always cut out the stencil with the shiny side up. It's easier to cut on the shiny side and easier to see the pattern through.

Materials

- Electric stencil cutting pen with the tip of your choice*
- 11" x 16" piece of clear glass
- Mylar
- Patterns (any clipart, coloring book art or original designs)
- Masking or clear tape
- Permanent black marking pen
- Pliers

* Used in this example: Electric Stencil Cutting Pen by Wall Lenk

1 Select the tip you will be using for cutting and screw it into the electric stencil cutting pen. Secure it with pliers (do not over-tighten). Plug the pen into a 120V AC power outlet (standard home outlet) and allow it to heat up for about five minutes.

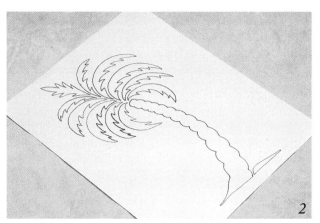

2 Place the pattern face up on a flat work surface.

3 Place the Mylar shiny side up on top of the glass. Align the Mylar over the designs, allowing for at least a 1" border around the designs. Secure the Mylar with a few pieces of tape.

4 Transfer any reference markings onto the Mylar using a black marking pen.

5 Cut out all areas (windows) to be stenciled with the electric stencil cutting pen. To cut, move the pen slowly as if tracing the pattern. Apply only a light pressure and keep the pen on the Mylar surface.

6 The cut areas will be easy to remove with your fingers or a pointed tool when the Mylar is lifted up from the glass.

7 When the electric stencil cutting pen is not being used, place the tool on the wire stand. When you are finished cutting, unplug the tool, allow it to cool, then remove the tip using pliers.

Tips
- Tighten the tip in the pen with pliers prior to use. Do not over-tighten. Always loosen the tip after each use to prevent it from "freezing" in the pen. To clean off residue or to re-sharpen the point of the tip, very gently brush the tip with fine emery cloth or 0000 steel wool.
- Caution: Grip the handle only. Do not touch any metal parts; hot pens can cause severe burns. Use it carefully. Always rest the tip on the holder and unplug it after use. Keep it away from combustible materials. And, as always, keep it away from children.

Basic Stenciling Instructions

Stenciling requires only a few basic tools and some simple how-to instructions. Here are the basics for mastering the technique.

Stencil brushes

The most common stencil brushes are flat-tipped and domed brushes with bristles bound tightly in a circle. They come in different sizes for different projects. Flat-tipped brushes contain bristles that are all one length. Domed brushes have bristles that are slightly tapered near the ends. A double ended stencil brush will have two brush heads and is easy to use when applying more than one color. Rather than stopping to clean the first color of paint from the brush, it can be flipped over and the second head can be used to apply the next color.

Small brushes are best when used with stencils that have smaller cut-out areas. Large brushes should be used with larger cut-out areas.

Stenciling on fabric

Prewash fabrics to remove the sizing. Mix acrylic paints with textile medium in a ratio of about 50/50 or use textile paints for stenciling. Fabrics take paint faster than walls or furniture, so it's important to swirl off paint on paper towels prior to stenciling. Stencil using the instructions above. Allow the stenciled fabric to dry for ten days before washing.

Cleaning stencils and stencil brushes

Remove as much paint as possible with a paper towel. Clean stencils and stencil brushes with dish detergent and warm water. Rinse them throroughly and let dry. You may also use a commercial stencil brush cleaning solution, following the manufacturer's instructions.

Stenciling tips

If you're a beginner, try a test run of the stenciling technique on a practice board or piece of fabric. It will help in knowing how much paint to use on the brush.

Lift the stencil during your stenciling to check the amount of paint you're applying. The tendency is to apply too much paint; you can always reapply color for greater intensity.

Occasionally clean off paint build-up on stencils with a clean, damp sponge.

When using stencils with more than one overlay, be sure to place a pencil dot in the registration marks and match up the marks when positioning the overlays.

Designer **Secrets**

Surfaces to be stenciled should be free from grease, dirt and other obvious marks. Painted surfaces can be of the following sheens: flat, eggshell, stain, low-luster or semi-gloss. High-gloss surfaces are more difficult to stencil on and may require light sanding or a surface preparation product prior to stenciling.

Materials

- Masking tape, painter's blue tape or stencil adhesive spray
- Stencil brushes
- Acrylic paint
- Paper or plastic plate
- Paper towels
- Instructions

1 Secure the stencil to the surface with small pieces of tape or use repositional stencil adhesive spray, following the manufacturer's instructions.

2 Pour small amount of acrylic paints onto the paper or plastic plate.

3 Consider the first rule of stenciling: Less is more. Successful stenciling is done in a dry brush technique. Lightly dab the stencil brush in the paint and swirl off the excess on a paper towel.

4 Holding the brush straight up and down, use a circular motion to apply a small amount of paint to the cutouts of the stencil. Use a separate stencil brush for each different color family. Use the stencil brush to apply more color (darker) around the edges of the stencil. Use lighter pressure to apply less or lighter color near the center. Stenciling a design darker will give it the appearance of being closer. Stenciling lighter will make the design appear further away as in the case of petals, leaves and vines.

5 To keep one color from going into another cut-out area, apply small pieces of tape to block off adjacent areas.

6 Allow the finished product to dry completely.

Making Framed **Canvas Panels**

Materials

- Four wood stretcher bars (purchased in pairs from craft or art supply stores in the appropriate sizes for the length and width of the panels)
- Primed or unprimed canvas
- Staple gun and heavy-duty staples (or hammer and tacks)
- Scissors or rotary cutter and mat
- Measuring tape
- Straight edge
- T-square
- Rubber mallet
- Framed Canvas Corner Panel Template (see page 136)

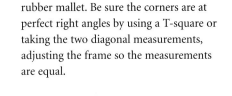

1 Join the corners of the four stretcher bars by pushing them together by hand. If necessary, tap them lightly with a rubber mallet. Be sure the corners are at perfect right angles by using a T-square or taking the two diagonal measurements, adjusting the frame so the measurements are equal.

2 Place the canvas, primed side down, onto a clean, flat surface. Place the frame on top of the canvas.

3 Measure and mark the canvas 3" wider than the frame all the way around.

4 Cut out the canvas using a scissors or rotary cutter and mat. At the corners, cut the canvas according to the template (see page 136).

Designer **Secrets**

- If the frame of the panel is larger than 40", add wood braces for additional support. Smooth any imperfections in the stretcher bars with a piece of fine sandpaper. You can make your own stretchers from 1" x 2" wood, mitering the corners and joining them with corrugated nails. Canvas pliers are available to help pull the canvas tight; or enlist the help of a friend to do the pulling while you staple.
- Do not wet the back of primed canvas. If you wish to prime your own canvas, use gesso applied with a 2" nylon brush. Dampen the bristles of the brush before loading with gesso. Apply two coats of gesso, the first coat in one direction (horizontally), and, when dry, apply the second coat in the opposite direction (vertically). The gesso will provide a chalky finish and paint colors will appear brighter.

5 Place the frame again, centering it in the middle of the cut canvas. Fold up the side to be sure the corners will meet.

6 The most important part for achieving a taut, evenly stretched canvas is to work from the center of each side out toward the corners and to work on opposite sides.

7 In the middle of the top stretcher bar, pull the canvas over the stretcher bar toward the back. Using the staple gun, put one staple through the canvas in the middle of the top stretcher bar. Keeping the canvas in position, pull the canvas over the opposite side stretcher bar and put a staple in the middle of the stretcher bar. Pull the canvas on one adjacent side over the stretcher bar and staple in the center. Repeat with the fourth side.

8 Working from the center of each side out toward each corner, staple the canvas to the back of the stretcher bars, pulling the canvas as tightly as possible. Continue working on opposite sides. Work to within 2" of each corner.

9 At the corners, fold the corners of the canvas in and staple. Trim any excess canvas close to the stretcher bars.

Enlarging a Pattern

There are a few effective ways to enlarge a pattern or design from a book. Two of the methods you use will depend on the access you have to a commercial copy center or a computer. The old-fashioned grid method using a pencil and ruler can be used anytime.

Commercial copy center

The easiest way to enlarge a pattern is to take it to a copy center and have it photocopied on a copy machine. Technicians can enlarge your pattern to whatever size you need, even taking 8½" x 11" paper to poster size.

Some copy centers have self-service machines that you can use yourself. Simply dial the percentage increase you need and push the copy button. Specific directions for machine use will be provided at the individual copy centers.

Costs range from a few pennies to a few dollars, depending on the services provided. You might want to have multiple copies made while you're there to save time.

Computer

Option two requires a computer, printer, scanner (or digital camera) and some drawing software. Scan the pattern to get it into the computer, then enlarge it to the required size using appropriate software. Print out the image and save it so you can print additional copies if you want them later.

Some software programs have a multipage option that will automatically print all the pages you need to fit your design together. With others, you will have to break up the image into a size your printer can handle. Then tape the pages together to make the larger image. Adobe Photoshop, Jasc PaintShop and SG Designs Rapid Resizer are a few software programs that work well.

Grid method

This is also known as graphic interpolation. Draw a grid across the original picture (or lay transparent graph paper over it). Draw a grid with larger squares on a second sheet of paper the size you want your final project to be. If you want the final drawing to be twice as large as the original, make your grid squares twice as large as the squares on the original grid. Copy the image square by square to the enlarged grid by drawing what you see in each square. Work one square at a time.

To enlarge an image that is larger than the paper, follow the directions for the grid method, drawing as much as you can fit on one sheet of paper. Move to the next quadrant, draw as much as you can fit, and continue until the entire pattern is drawn. Tape the pages together.

Chapter

Bamboo and
Palm Trees

Warm tropical breezes, flowing palm trees and lush vegetation all help to conjure up the inviting images of an *exotic* island getaway. In this chapter, you'll be able to set your dream in motion.

The airy silk fern leaves provide the basis for the *Tropical* Leaf Wall Hanging. When they're first covered with an inexpensive joint compound and then painted, they take on a pricey designer look for a fraction of the cost. By simply hinging three canvas framed panels together and adding some *wonderful* palm tree prints, the Tri-fold Screen can hide that unsightly clutter. The bamboo legs are really wooden dowels with beads of joint compound added to simulate the boney "knuckles" found in nature.

Add a couple of Palm Tree Pillows, made with some easy rub-ons, and get ready to kick back with a piña colada.

Tri-Fold Screen
with Faux Bamboo Legs

Folding screens or room dividers are useful in many areas of a home. They define a space and add color, *texture,* and height. This project incorporates texture not only in the painting technique, but also with the use of brass tacks and faux bamboo legs. Even the bamboo legs add an element of *surprise*. They're really made from wooden dowels.

Materials

- 3 framed canvas panels, 12" x 48"
- 6 wooden dowels, 12" long, ¾" diameter (or 2 dowels 36" long, ¾" diameter, cut into 12" lengths)
- Joint compound (tube form)
- 2 piano hinges (36" long) or 4 folding screen hinges and associated hardware
- 3 packages standard brass upholstery tacks
- 6 double end screws
- Acrylic paint*: 2 oz. each light parchment, antique green, celery green, caramel, heritage brick, raw umber and 8 oz. taffy cream
- Clear satin finish (spray or wipe-on)
- ½" foam brush
- 1½" foam brush
- Mini-foam roller
- 1½" chip brush
- Painter's blue tape (1" wide)

- Double ended stencil brush (clean after use)*
- 200-grit sandpaper
- Bucket of sand or block of Styrofoam
- Tack cloth
- Cotton cloths
- Paper towels
- Paper or plastic plate
- Measuring tape
- Pencil
- Hand saw
- Screwdriver
- Hammer
- Power drill with ⅛" bit
- Water
- Safety glasses
- * Used in this project: Stencil Ease Double Ended Stencil Brush, DecoArt Americana Acrylic Paints

Note: Canvas panels can either be purchased or made according to the instructions on page 19.

Designer Secrets

Determine the way you would like the folding screen to fold prior to the installation of the hinges. Take a piece of paper and fold it in thirds lengthwise to help you decide the folding layout.

1 If you purchased dowels with the longer length, cut them down to 12" using the hand saw. Sand the six dowels with 200-grit sandpaper until smooth. Remove the sanding dust with a tack cloth or clean cotton cloth.

2 On each wood dowel leg, add knuckle joints found naturally on bamboo stalks by applying a bead of joint compound around the dowel. Apply a second bead of joint compound right next to the first bead. Sculpt the joint compound with your fingers, tapering it to a thin, feathered edge. Make two knuckle joints on each piece of dowel.

3 Place the ends of the dowels into a bucket of sand or block of Styrofoam and let dry for several hours or overnight until the joint compound has completely set up.

4 Paint the dowels with one coat of light parchment acrylic paint using ½" foam brush. Let dry. Lightly sand the dowels with 200-grit sandpaper when the paint is dry.

Tip Double ended stencil brushes are handy to flip back and forth so you don't have to stop to clean a brush when using two colors. Either end can be used.

5 Squeeze a small amount of antique green onto a paper or plastic plate. Dip the stencil brush into the paint and swirl it across paper towels to remove most of the paint. Dry brush the antique green color onto the dowels. Let dry.

6 Squeeze a small amount of celery green acrylic paint onto a paper or plastic plate. Dip the stencil brush into the paint and swirl it across paper towels to remove most of the paint. Dry brush the celery green color on the dowels. Let dry. When dry brushing, the paint tends to "collect" in and define the raised joint areas.

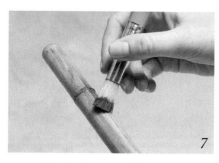

7 Dip the clean stencil brush into raw umber acrylic paint and dry brush on the dowels. Let dry.

8 Seal the painted dowels with clear satin acrylic spray or the wipe-on version of same product. Set aside the faux bamboo legs.

9 For the canvas screen panels, make or purchase three canvas panels 12" x 48". (Follow the instructions on page 19 if you choose to make your own panels.)

10 Paint each panel front and side with taffy cream acrylic paint using a mini foam roller. Let dry.

11 Measure the borders for each panel of the screen with a measuring tape. On the two end panels, the top border measures 1½", the bottom border measures 2" and the side borders measure 1". For the center panel, measure 1½" for the top border and 2" for the bottom border. The center panel has no side borders. Using painter's blue tape, mask off the interior of each screen by placing the tape along the outer edge of the borders.

12 Squeeze a small amount of caramel acrylic paint onto a paper or plastic plate. Dip a 1½" chip brush into the paint and remove most of the paint by swirling it over paper towels. Dry brush the interior portion of the panel. Let dry. Remove the tape.

13 Place painter's blue tape along the border line over the paint just applied to the inside panel. Squeeze a small amount of heritage brick acrylic paint onto a paper or plastic plate. Paint the border using a ½" foam brush. Let dry. Remove the tape. Thin the paint with a small amount of water to the consistency of skim milk. Dip the 1½" foam brush into the mixture and drag it down the sides of the panels in a stria method (see page 12). Let dry and remove the tape. Reload the brush as needed and smooth overlapping brush strokes in the same stria method.

14 Hammer the upholstery tacks in the border areas of each panel spacing them 1" apart.

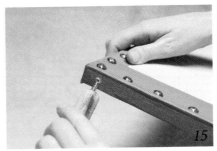

15 Wearing safety glasses, drill holes in one end of each faux bamboo leg with the ⅛" bit.

Screw one end of a double ended screw into each leg. Drill two holes into the bottom of each canvas panel frame close to the sides and screw the other end of the legs into the frames. Each panel will have two legs.

16 Line up the three screen panels face-down next to each other, positioning the end panels on either side of the center panel. Position the piano hinges along the back of one frame and the side edge of the adjacent frame so they open in the opposite direction in a zigzag fashion.

After marking the location of the screw holes, pre-drill the holes for the piano hinge screws. Screw the piano hinges in place.

Palm Tree Panels

The *tropical* look is very popular in home décor. We love the look of palm trees because it takes us far away from the busy schedules of our daily lives. We can almost feel the ocean *breeze* gently blowing through the palm leaves. These panels added to the folding screen are almost like artwork hanging on the walls. They make a statement in a casually stylish way.

Materials

- 3 primed, framed canvas panels 8" x 16"
- Palm tree pattern (see page 139)
- Mylar
- Electric stencil cutting pen*
- Acrylic paint*: 2 oz. each Hauser green light, Hauser green umber, light red oxide and 8 oz. wedgewood green
- Joint compound
- 2" foam brush
- 2 stencil brushes (½") or 1

double ended stencil brush
- Painter's blue tape (1" wide)
- Plastic putty knife or old credit card
- Paper or plastic plate
- Paper towels
- * Used in this project: Electric Stencil Cutting Pen by Wall Lenk, Plaid FolkArt Acrylic Paint, Delta Ceramcoat Acrylic Paint

Designer **Secrets**

Attach the palm tree panels to the folding screen using hook and loop tape or heavy-duty double-sided foam tape. Because they are not permanently attached, you can remove the panels for a different look in your home.

1 Purchase three 8" x 16" framed canvas panels. (Follow the instructions on page 19 if you are making your own panels.)

2

2 Paint the canvas panel fronts and sides with wedgewood green acrylic paint using a foam brush. Let dry.

3 Use the palm tree stencil pattern to cut your own stencil from Mylar with the electric stencil cutting pen (see page 16).

4 Lay the stencil onto the canvas panel, centering the design vertically and tape it in place using a few small pieces of painter's blue tape on the top and bottom of the stencil.

5 Apply a coat of joint compound over the stencil using a plastic putty knife or an old credit card. Smooth the joint compound over the top of the stencil. Carefully remove the tape and gently lift the stencil straight up, disturbing the joint compound as little as possible. Immediately clean the stencil with soapy water and dry it with paper towels. Let the joint compound dry for several hours. It will be dry to the touch in 30-40 minutes, but completely cured in three to four hours.

6 Place the clean stencil over the top of the canvas, lining it up with the dry, raised design. Tape the top of the stencil to the canvas using a piece of painter's blue tape. Pour small amounts of Hauser green umber and Hauser green light acrylic paint onto a paper or plastic plate. Dip a stencil brush into the Hauser green light paint and swirl it lightly over paper towels to remove excess paint. Apply the paint over the stencil to the leaf edges and the middle of the trunk. Do not cover the stencil completely.

7 Dip the same stencil brush into the Hauser green umber and dry brush off onto paper towels. Swirl the paint onto the palm tree leaves and trunk to add shadows and create depth in the stenciled design.

8 Squeeze a small amount of light red oxide acrylic paint onto a paper or plastic plate. Use a separate clean stencil brush to apply light red oxide to the palm tree flower and sparingly add accents of the color to the leaves and trunk. The paint will dry quickly.

9 Left up the stencil and clean it in soapy water.

Tips
- To eliminate any rough joint compound ridges, lightly sand with 200-grit sandpaper when dry. Shake off the dust and then stencil with paints.
- Reverse the stencil to make left- and right-facing palm trees.

Tropical Leaf Wall Hanging

When I thought up this project, I knew that I wanted *textured* dimensional leaves to attach to the painted canvas panel. I experimented with *different* mediums and techniques to create texture, then discovered the ever-useful chip brush. It's sturdy, inexpensive and takes a lot of abuse! Dabbing the joint compound onto the leaves requires a stiff brush!

Materials

- 24" x 24" primed canvas panel
- 3 silk or plastic fern leaves
- Joint compound
- Acrylic paint*: 2 oz. each Hauser green light and Hauser green umber
- Color spray*: lemon peel, clover and black
- Clear satin sealer, low-sheen
- 1½" chip brush
- 1½" foam brush
- Paper or plastic plate
- Aluminum pie pan or old plastic bowl
- Wax paper
- Paper towels
- Glue gun and glue sticks or white glue

* Used in this project: Duncan Tulip Cool Colors Spray, Plaid FolkArt Acrylic Paint

Designer **Secrets**

To keep the dried joint compound from flaking off, use a good spray sealer or matte finish.

1 Make or purchase one 24" x 24" canvas panel. (Follow the instructions on page 19 if your are making your own panel.)

2 Squeeze small amounts of Hauser green light and Hauser green umber paints onto a paper or plastic plate. Using the foam brush, pick up both colors, blending them together slightly. On the primed side of the canvas, apply the blended greens, adding more color to cover the entire canvas. Let dry.

3 Lay the silk or plastic fern leaves on wax paper. Dip the chip brush into the joint compound. Dab the compound over the front of the leaves. Flip them over and apply the joint compound to the back. The entire leaf front and back will be covered with joint compound. Don't smooth the joint compound because you want a textured look. Let dry.

4 Spray the leaves with clear satin sealer. Let dry.

5 Pour a small puddle of each of the color spray colors into an aluminum pie pan or old plastic bowl. Mix together the black and lemon peel to make a sage-type green. Mix the black and clover to make a darker green.

Tip Use a plastic plate with compartments to pour the colors into.

6 Use a foam brush to dab the colors onto the fronts of the leaves. It is not necessary to paint the backs. Blot the paint with paper towels to remove the excess. Let dry.

7 Glue the leaves onto the canvas using a glue gun and glue sticks or white glue. Refer to the picture for the arrangement of the leaves.

Palm Tree Pillow

If you have seen pillows like this in *trendy* boutiques, you know how pricey they can be. These pillows look like a million bucks! They have a *high-end* custom designer appearance, but can be made very affordably. This is what making your own home décor projects is all about for me ... creating something that did not cost a lot of money, took little time and was easy to do. Now, that's a good feeling, and you did it yourself!

Materials

- 1 yd. unprimed canvas fabric
- 10" x 10" primed canvas
- 14" x 14" pillow form
- Acrylic paint*: 2 oz. light parchment
- Rub-ons*: 4 palm trees and 4 botanical names
- 1" foam brush

- Scissors or rotary cutter and mat
- Wooden craft stick
- Sewing machine
- * Used in this project: Duncan Rub-On Transfer in Palms MPD300, DecoArt Americana Acrylic Paint

Designer **Secrets**

Choose a fringe or decorative trim in a color found in the rub-on design. Take the design to the fabric store for a perfect match and take the guesswork out of it.

1 Paint the 10" x 10" primed canvas with light parchment paint using the foam brush. Let dry.

2 Cut loosely around the rub-on palm trees and botanical names. Following the manufacturer's instructions, rub on the four palm trees and the botanical names using a wooden craft stick, referring to the picture for placement.

3 Lift up the Mylar to be sure all areas of the rub-on designs have been transferred.

4 Sew the painted panel to the front of the pillow, centering it on the pillow.

Sew your own **pillow cover**

1 Cut one canvas piece 16" square for the front of the pillow. Cut two pieces of canvas 16" x 10" for the back.

2 Sew ¼" double-folded hem on the 10" side of each of the back panels.

3 Stitch, overlapping the back panel together at the top and bottom.

4 Sew the trim around the outside edge of the pillow front. Be sure the trim is facing in, toward the center of the pillow.

5 Place the pillow front and back pieces right sides together with the hemmed edges of the back pieces overlapping each other. Stitch around all four sides.

6 Turn the pillow right-side out. Insert the pillow form into the back opening.

Chapter ④

Faux Leather
and Animal Print

The rich look of leather combined with animal prints is the definition of masculine elegance.

The *realistic* look of the Faux Leather Pillows is guaranteed to keep the heads turning. Try all three versions, toss them on a sofa or chair, and it'll look like you just returned from your own *private safari*. Mention crocodile and watch prices skyrocket. I came up with an incredible faux crocodile look on the box by just using a stencil, joint compound and stain. Your friends will be impressed—decorators will be green with envy. To tie my "call of the wild" look together, I trimmed lampshades and trays with fun animal print bands. The stencil patterns are included in the book. Stencils are also the main ingredient used in the Overlapping Floorcloth. Even though it's just one piece of canvas, the stunning effect makes it look like three separate rugs tossed together.

Who needs a green thumb when you can make *amazing* and realistic looking tropical plants with some canvas and a little acrylic paint? Paste wax is the secret behind the glossy shine on the life-like leaves.

Try these accessories for an upscale appearance in your den, study or office. Nobody will believe it all started with simple canvas.

Overlapping **Floorcloth**

Incorporating trompe l' oeil (fool the eye painting techniques) with *faux finishing* is one of my favorite decorative painting objectives. This floorcloth really does look like it is three separate floorcloths overlapping one another, yet it was all done on one piece. With a bit of painting trickery, you'll have everyone doing a *double-take*. And it's all done with just canvas and paint!

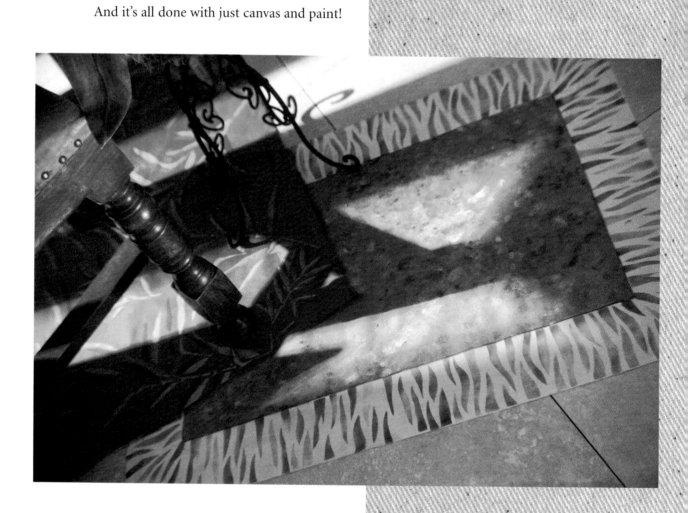

Materials

- Double primed canvas (see sizing in Steps 1 and 2)
- 8½" x 11" Mylar
- 10" x 12" piece of glass
- 3 stencil brushes (½")
- Electric stencil cutting pen* or craft knife
- Artist liner brush
- Acrylic paint*: 2 oz. each caramel, charcoal, light parchment, khaki tan, neutral grey, celery green, avocado, black, wash white, raw umber, burnt umber and tomato red
- Mini foam roller
- 1" foam brush
- 2" foam brush
- Measuring tape or yard stick
- Pencil
- Scissors
- Paper or plastic plate
- Painter's blue tape (1" wide)
- Heavy-duty tacky glue* or heavy-duty tape

- Satin or gloss acrylic finish
- Craft paper
- Paper towels
- Table knife
- Bamboo pattern (see page 137)
- Zebra pattern (see page 133)
- * Used in this project: Electric Stencil Cutting Pen by Wall Lenk, Crafter's Pick "The Ultimate," DecoArt Americana Acrylic Paint
- Note: Follow the stencil cutting instructions on page 16 to cut the bamboo and zebra stencils.

1 To determine the layout of the overlapping floorcloth, cut three pieces of craft paper the size you want each floorcloth to be. My three pieces measured 20" x 30" each. Arrange the three pieces as pictured, scattered end to end, overlapping slightly. Tape the pieces together to make the craft paper template.

2 Place the craft paper template on the canvas and trace around it. Add 1½" for the hem around the outside of the floorcloth. Cut out the floorcloth on the outside line.

3 Mark 4½" borders around all floorcloths. Tape off the inside and outside edges of the borders using painter's blue tape. This includes a 1" hem that will be turned under.

4

4 Base paint the three borders in caramel, khaki tan and light parchment paint using mini rollers or foam brushes. Refer to the photo for color placement.

Designer **Secrets**

To enable us to get close-up photos and show detail on this project, the how-to photographs were taken using a floorcloth that was reduced in size. However, after creating the smaller version of the floorcloth, I found that this size worked very well as a table runner!

5 To measure and mark for diamonds, draw a light pencil line from the upper right corner to the bottom left corner, doing the same for the opposite side, making an "X." Measure and mark off parallel lines 4" apart to make the diamonds. There will be partial diamonds all around the edges.

6 Tape off the diamonds to paint, or paint the diamonds freehand using a foam brush. Paint half of the diamonds with avocado acrylic paint. Use a liner artist brush dipped in a thinned mixture of water and avocado to outline the light diamonds (left unpainted on the canvas).

7 When the paint has dried, tape around the borders on the inside edges. Paint in these areas using ¾ tomato red paint mixed with about ¼ burnt umber inside the caramel border. Use the celery green and avocado paints inside the khaki tan border to paint every other diamond. Alternate the colors. Use raw umber paint inside the light parchment border.

8 To paint the multicolored center in the light parchment-bordered section, first paint the center in raw umber. While the paint is tacky, squeeze drops of caramel, khaki tan and light parchment randomly over the center. Use a mini roller to roll over all the drops of paint until the desired look is achieved.

9 Squeeze raw umber and caramel paints onto a paper or plastic plate. Dip a stencil brush into the caramel paint and remove excess paint by wiping the brush over paper towels. Stencil the zebra design on the light parchment border. Stencil with variations of raw umber and caramel mixed together to create interest in the design.

10 Stencil the bamboo with light parchment paint. Repeat the process, adding bamboo motifs over the entire tomato red area.

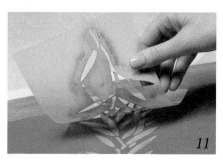

11 Lift up the bamboo stencil to check your work. It is better not to solidly color in the entire stencil area, leaving some background color in the center of the stencil to add color to the bamboo.

12 Position the stencil over the top of each motif. Using avocado and celery green acrylic paints, add a little color to the bamboo leaves and stems using a stencil brush.

13 Slightly offset the stencil over each motif and lightly add neutral grey shadows using a stencil brush. Overlap the stencil slightly onto the stenciled bamboo leaves to add shading.

14 For the spotted center area, squeeze dots of wash white, black and raw umber paint directly onto the area.

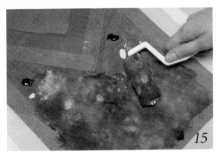

15 Using a dampened mini foam roller (wet the roller and squeeze out all the water), smudge the paint by rolling over it in all different directions until you get the look you desire. No two areas will ever look the same. Just be sure not to over-roll the area so that it becomes muddy.

16 Apply painter's blue tape over the caramel-colored border where the floorcloths appear to overlap each other. Use neutral grey paint and a stencil brush to stencil a shadow along the edge, adding dimension and emphasis to the appearance of the overlapping pieces of fabric.

17 Remove the tape to reveal the shadow.

18 Fold under a 1" hemline and crease with the backside of a dull knife. Clip the corners diagonally with scissors to reduce bulk. This will enable the sides to fold in and meet at a mitered corner. Clip any other hem area of the floorcloth that needs to be cut in order to fold the hem under.

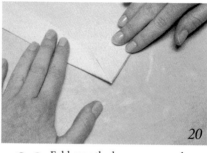

20 Fold over the hem, crease and press. You may want to lay a heavy object on the hem until the glue sets. Often times, I place wax paper over the glued area and then lay books on top of the wax paper to protect the books from the glue.

19 Use heavy-duty tacky glue where you will fold the hem over.

21 Apply several coats of satin or gloss acrylic finish to the entire surface, letting each coat dry before applying the next. I used pint-sized clear acrylic finish and applied it with a foam brush. Let dry.

This overlapping floorcloth has countless possibilities. Add more sections, different colors, and new stencils to create your own masterpiece for every room in the house.

Leather-Look Canvas Pillows

I've been creating faux finishes since the word faux was pronounced "fox"! However, faux finishes have been around since the Egyptians, or even before, I suspect, and therefore, I can't take credit for anything other than educating someone on the correct way to pronounce faux.

Having done faux for years, I try to come up with *new* ways to create copy finishes of the "real thing." Leather is often imitated on walls. I *experimented* with different colors, materials and tools until I came up with my version of faux leather on primed canvas.

Designer **Secrets**
It really is ALL in the colors of paint used. Sticking with these colors will ensure that you achieve a realistic look. After all, would we really think it was faux leather if the canvas was painted lavender?

Red **Pillow**

Designer **Secrets**
Fold wax paper around the band and then lay a weight on top. If any of the glue seeps out as the glue dries, it will not stick to the wax paper and will peel off easily.

Materials

- ½ yd. primed canvas (54" wide)
- 5" square of suede in a beige or natural color
- 12" pillow form
- Acrylic paint*: 2 oz. each tomato red, burnt umber and honey brown
- Wood stain*
- 6 decorative beads
- Painter's blue tape (1" wide)
- Plastic grocery bags
- Paper towels
- Brown craft paper or wax paper
- Disposable latex gloves
- Mini foam roller
- 2 foam brushes (1½")
- Kitchen table knife
- Heavy-duty tacky glue*

- Glue gun and hot glue sticks
- Sewing machine
- Scissors or rotary cutter and mat
- Measuring tape
- Pencil
- * Used in this project: Minwax Provincial Wood Stain, Crafter's Pick "The Ultimate," DecoArt Americana Acrylic Paint

1 Cut three pieces of primed canvas 1" larger than the pillow form dimensions (13" x 13"). Two pieces will be used to create an opening in the back to stuff the pillow form.

2 Cut two strips of canvas 2" x 14½" for the decorative bands.

3 On the primed side, paint all three pillow pieces with a mixture of ⅔ tomato red to ⅓ burnt umber using the mini foam roller.

4 While the paint is still wet, press a scrunched plastic bag over the paint, dabbing the paint to distress the look. Allow to dry.

5 Paint the pillow bands with honey brown using a foam brush. While the paint is still wet, press a scrunched plastic bag over the paint, dabbing it to create a distressed look. Let dry.

6 Place the painted canvas on a work surface covered with brown craft paper or wax paper. Wearing disposable gloves, apply a thin coat of wood stain with a foam brush over the red paint. While the stain is still wet, lay a plastic grocery bag onto the surface and scrunch it down. Lift the plastic up. Some of the stain will be removed and some will remain. Dab the stain with the plastic bag until you are pleased with the appearance. If needed, remove excess stain by gently blotting with a paper towel. Allow to dry flat for 24 hours.

7 Fold the pillow bands in thirds lengthwise with right sides out. Crease them with your hands or with the dull side of a table knife.

8 Glue the bands together lengthwise with wrong sides together using heavy-duty tacky glue. Let the glue dry.

9 Place the bands on the front of the pillow (⅓ in from each side) and stitch them at the top and bottom with a sewing machine ¼" from the edge.

10 For the back, fold under one edge of each of the two ack pieces ½", then fold them under again 1". Topstitch a hem close to the folded edge.

11 Place the front of the pillow right-side up. Place the two back pieces on top of the front, right sides together, with the hemmed edges overlapping each other. Stitch around all four sides using ½" seam allowance. Turn the pillow right-side out. Insert the pillow form into the back opening.

12 Hot glue the decorative beads on the front bands.

4-Square **Divided Pillow**

Materials

- ½ yd. primed canvas (54" wide)
- 12" pillow form
- Acrylic paint*: 2 oz. each tomato red, burnt umber and moon yellow
- Wood stain*
- Painter's blue tape (1" wide)
- Plastic grocery bags
- Paper towels
- Disposable latex gloves
- Heavy-duty tacky glue*
- 2 foam brushes (1½")

- Sewing machine
- Scissors or rotary cutter and mat
- Measuring tape
- Pencil
- * Used in this project: Minwax Provincial Wood Stain, Crafter's Pick "The Ultimate," DecoArt Americana Acrylic Paint

1 Cut three pieces of primed canvas 1" larger than the pillow form (13" x 13"). Two pieces will be used to create an opening in the back to stuff the pillow form.

2

2 For the front of the pillow, divide the primed side of the canvas into four equal squares. Tape off the squares in diagonal corners by placing painter's blue tape along the center lines. Paint with a mixture of ⅔ tomato red and ⅓ burnt umber using a foam brush. Let dry and remove the tape.

3

3 Tape off the two remaining squares and paint them moon yellow using a foam brush. Let dry and remove the tape.

4 Place the painted canvas on a work surface covered with brown craft paper or wax paper. Wearing disposable gloves, apply a thin coat of wood stain with a foam brush over the painted squares. While the stain is still wet, place a plastic grocery bag onto the surface and scrunch it down. Dab the stain with the plastic bag until you are pleased with the appearance. If needed, remove the excess stain by gently blotting with a paper towel. Allow it to dry flat for 24 hours.

5 For the back, fold under one edge of each of the two back pieces ½", then fold them under again 1". Topstitch a hem close to the folded edges on each piece.

6 Turn the pillow front right-side up. Place the two back pieces on the front, right sides together, overlapping the hemmed edges. Stitch around all four sides using ½" seam allowance. Turn the pillow cover right-side out. Insert the pillow form in the back opening.

Antique Green Pillow
with Suede Trim

Materials

- ½ yd. primed canvas (54" wide)
- 6" x 6" primed canvas
- 4 pieces 2" x 6" tan suede fabric
- 12" pillow form
- Acrylic paint*: 2 oz. each antique green and camel brown
- Wood stain*
- Painter's blue tape (1" wide)
- Plastic grocery bags
- Paper towels
- Brown craft paper or wax paper
- Disposable latex gloves
- Heavy-duty tacky glue*

- 1½" foam brush
- Sea sponge
- Sewing machine
- Scissors or rotary cutter and mat
- Measuring tape
- Pencil
- * Used in this project: Minwax Provincial Wood Stain, Crafter's Pick "The Ultimate," DecoArt Americana Acrylic Paint

1 Cut three pieces of primed canvas 1" larger than the pillow form (13" x 13"). Two pieces will be used to create an opening in the back to stuff the pillow form.

2 Paint the three large canvas pieces antique green using a dampened sea sponge to dab the color onto the primed side of the canvas. Allow the pieces to dry. Wash the sea sponge and squeeze out all of the water.

3 Use the sea sponge to paint the 6" square canvas with camel brown acrylic paint. Allow the 6" square to dry.

4 Place the painted canvas on a work surface covered with brown craft paper or wax paper. Wearing disposable gloves, apply a thin coat of wood stain with a foam brush over the antique green paint. While the stain is still wet, lay a plastic grocery bag on the surface and scrunch it down. Lift the plastic up. Some of the stain will be removed and some will remain. Dab the stain with the plastic bag until you are pleased with the appearance. If needed, remove the excess stain by gently blotting with a paper towel. Allow the canvas to dry flat for 24 hours.

5 Repeat Step 4 for the 6" square canvas. Let it dry for 24 hours.

6 Using scissors, cut narrow fringe along the length of one side of each of the suede strips to within ¼" of the opposite edge.

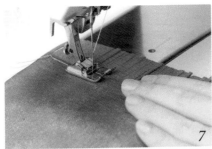

7 Sew one suede fringe strip to the back edge of each side of the 6" square. Sew or glue the fringed square diagonally on the pillow front.

8 For the back, fold under one edge of each of the two back pieces ½", then fold them under again 1". Topstitch a hem close to the folded edges.

9 Turn the pillow front right-side up. Place the two back pieces on the front, right sides together, overlapping the hemmed edges. Stitch around all four sides using ½" seam allowance. Turn the pillow right-side out. Insert the pillow form in the back opening.

Yellow **Diamond Pillow**

Materials

- ½ yd. primed canvas (54" wide)
- 12" pillow form
- Decorative button
- Acrylic paint*: 2 oz. each light parchment and moon yellow
- Wood stain*
- Painter's blue tape (1" wide)
- Plastic grocery bags
- Paper towels
- Disposable latex gloves
- 2 foam brushes (1½")
- Sewing machine
- Scissors or rotary cutter and mat
- Measuring tape
- Pencil
- * Used in this project: Minwax Provincial Wood Stain, DecoArt Americana Acrylic Paint

1 Cut three pieces of primed canvas 1" larger than the pillow form (13" x 13"). Two pieces will be used to create an opening in the back to stuff the pillow form.

2 On the primed side, divide the canvas into four triangles by drawing a line from the upper left corner to the opposite corner at the lower right. Repeat for the other corners. Tape off every other triangle. Paint the two opposite triangles moon yellow using a foam brush. Dab the paint with a scrunched plastic bag to give it a distressed look until you are satisfied with the appearance. Paint the opposite corners light parchment.

3 Place the painted canvas on a work surface covered with brown craft paper or wax paper. Wearing disposable gloves, apply a thin coat of wood stain with a foam brush over the paint. While the stain is still wet, lay a plastic grocery bag on the surface and scrunch it down. Lift the plastic up. Some of the stain will be removed and some will remain. Dab the stain with the plastic bag until you are pleased with the appearance. If needed, remove the excess stain by gently blotting with a paper towel. Allow the canvas to dry flat for 24 hours.

4 For the back, fold under one edge of each of the two back pieces ½", then fold them under again 1". Topstitch a hem close to the folded edges on each piece.

5 Turn the pillow front right-side up. Place the two back pieces on the front, right sides together, overlapping the hemmed edges. Stitch around all four sides using ½" seam allowance. Turn the pillow cover right-side out. Insert the pillow form in the back opening.

Faux Crocodile Box

This project comes under my heading, "I wonder if I can imitate that texture?" Of course, that answer is always, *"why not!"* As a stencil designer, the crocodile stencil was the easy part. The next step in imitating faux crocodile was to work on the raised texture look. This was easy, too. The "unexpected happy accident," as I call all *good things* that come out of "mistakes," was to find that when the joint compound was stained with various colors of wood stain, it took on the appearance of crocodile skin—and no animals were harmed!

Materials

- Wood box*
- Primed canvas (see Steps 2 and 3 for the sizing of the canvas)
- Joint compound
- 8" x 11" Mylar sheet
- Craft knife
- Crocodile pattern (see page 135)
- Acrylic paint*: 8 oz. burnt sienna
- Oil-based wood stain*: oak and provincial
- 220-grit sandpaper

- Heavy-duty tacky glue*
- 2 foam brushes (2")
- Plastic putty knife
- Painter's blue tape (1" wide)
- Cotton cloths or paper towels
- Rubber gloves
- * Used in this project: Walnut Hollow Box #3213, Minwax Medium Oak Oil-Based Wood Stain, Minwax Provincial Oil-Based Wood Stain, Aleene's Heavy Duty Tacky Glue, DecoArt Americana Acrylic Paint

1 Using the Mylar, a craft knife and the crocodile pattern, make your own crocodile stencil (see page 16).

2 Measure the top and sides of the wood box. Draw these measurements on the primed canvas.

Tip Lay the box on the canvas and trace around it for quick measurements of the top and sides.

3 Cut the primed canvas pieces according to your measurements.

4 Paint the primed side of the canvas with burnt sienna acrylic paint using a foam brush. There's no need to be careful. Random brush strokes actually add more interest to the finished panel.

5 Lay the crocodile stencil on top of the canvas panel. You can tape it in place if you wish using painter's blue tape. Apply a coat of joint compound over the stencil using a plastic putty knife. Smooth the joint compound over the top of the stencil using the putty knife.

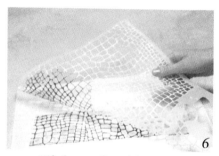

6 Lift the stencil straight up, disturbing the joint compound as little as possible. If you need to fill in any adjacent areas with joint compound, allow the first area to dry and then reposition the stencil next to the first area. Immediately clean the stencil in soapy water if you will not be using it again quickly. The joint compound should be dry to the touch within 30 to 40 minutes. It completely cures in four to six hours.

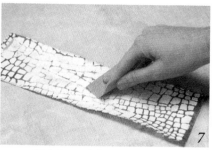

7 Lightly sand the panel with 220-grit sandpaper after 30 to 40 minutes or when dry. Remove the sanding dust using a clean cotton cloth.

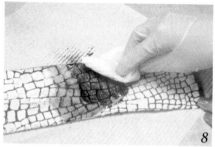

8 Put on gloves and work in a well-ventilated area. Apply the oak oil-based wood stain to the canvas panel using a cotton cloth or thick paper towels.

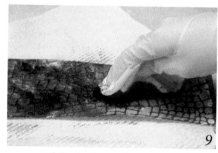

9 While the first stain is wet, apply the provincial oil-based wood stain with a cotton cloth or paper towel. Blot the stained panel to give it an uneven stained look. Let the canvas panel dry at least 24 hours in a well-ventilated area.

10 Spread the heavy-duty tacky glue evenly on the top of the box using a plastic putty knife.

12 Repeat this process on all four sides of the box.

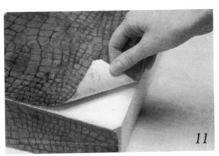

11 Align the crocodile piece on the top of the box with the edges and press down with your hands.

Tip • Cover the bottom of the box with felt or suede.
• To cover any white-trimmed edges of the canvas panels, use wood stain pens or permanent markers in colors to match.

Canvas **Plant**

Even if you weren't born with a green thumb, it's easy to turn canvas and paint into fabulous foliage. The canvas leaves in this plant are so *realistic* you might be tempted to get out the watering can.

One day, I was outside thinking about what projects I could make out of canvas when I caught myself looking at a plant. Not having any luck growing indoor *plants*, I came up with the idea of making a plant out of canvas—leaf by leaf. The results were amazing. Try different leaf shapes in different sizes.

Materials

- 1 yd. double-primed canvas (54" wide)
- Acrylic paint*: 2 oz. each Hauser green dark, Hauser green light, cream, burnt umber and plum
- Spray shellac or acrylic sealer
- Clear paste wax
- 22 feet of 18-gauge floral wire (12" to 18" per leaf, using 12 to 14 leaves)
- One ceramic or terra cotta plant container
- Floral foam, Styrofoam or sand
- Package of real dried moss
- Thick white glue

- Craft paper
- Wax paper
- 2 foam brushes (1")
- Soft cloth
- Plastic spatula or old credit card
- Paper or plastic plate
- Pencil
- Scissors
- Wire cutters
- Leaf pattern (see page 140)
- * Used in this project: Plaid FolkArt Acrylic Paint

Designer Secrets

When assembling the canvas plant, take a tip from nature. Most plants have a common stalk from which the leaves branch off. Pretend there is a center stalk in your canvas plant, too, and start placing the leaves in the middle of the container, working in a small circle around the planter. Add leaves to the outside of the circle as you build the plant. Also, using two different sizes of leaves gives the plant a more realistic look.

1 Using a pencil and craft paper, trace around the leaf patterns on page 140. Or if you prefer, trace around actual plant leaves. Vary the sizes of the leaf designs.

2 Cut out the paper leaf patterns, place them on the primed canvas, and trace around them. You will need a front and back for each leaf, so be sure to flip each leaf design pattern over so the front and back will match perfectly. Make 24-28.

3 Cut out the canvas leaves with scissors. Cut floral wire the length of each leaf plus 8" to 10" using wire cutters.

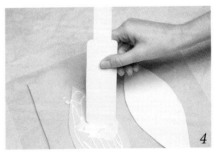

4 For each leaf, place the two matching front and back pieces primed side down onto wax paper. Apply thick white glue to each piece and distribute the glue over each piece with a plastic spatula or old credit card.

5 Center one wire down the length of one glue-covered leaf.

6 Place the matching leaf on top of the wire, sandwiching the wire inside. Fold wax paper over the leaf. Lay a heavy object on top of the leaf and wax paper. Repeat this step for each leaf. Dry flat overnight. The glue will not stick to the wax paper.

7 When the glue has dried, scrape off any excess glue on the edges of the leaves and trim any excess canvas that may not match perfectly.

8 Squeeze a small amount of each color of paint onto a paper or plastic plate. Using a foam brush, pick up the Hauser green light and Hauser green dark paints, mixing them slightly, and apply the paint to one side of the leaf. Cover the leaf with a blend of the green paints.

9 Using a clean foam brush, pick up some of the burnt umber and plum paints, mixing them slightly. Apply the paint on the center stem and blend it toward the outer edge of the leaf. Using a clean, dry foam brush, pick up some cream paint and highlight the center stem, blending out toward the edges. Remember that no two leaves are the same in nature; each painted leaf should look different. Stand the wire stems of the leaves in a tall heavy container to dry. Paint the other side of the leaves the same way and let dry. Repeat for each leaf.

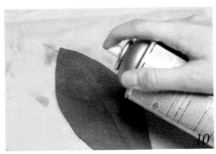

10 Spray both sides of each leaf with a thin coat of spray shellac or acrylic sealer. Let dry.

11 Apply a coat of clear paste wax to all leaves using a soft cloth. Let dry approximately 30 minutes, then buff with a clean cloth to a soft luster.

12 To assemble the plant, place floral foam, Styrofoam or sand into the bottom of the ceramic or terra cotta container. You may need to cut the foam into small square pieces to fit it snugly inside the container.

13 Insert the wire stems of the leaves into the foam, Styrofoam or sand. Gently bend the leaves in natural curves. Add moss to the top of the container to hide the foam, Styrofoam or sand.

Animal Print Band **Lampshade** and **Decorative Tray**

Constantly on the search for the *perfect* lampshade for my home décor clients, I found that plain shades are the most affordable, are readily available, offer a larger variety of sizes and shapes, and best of all, can be decorated to fit any room décor. Use this *technique* in an assortment of colors and designs to fit any home décor.

Designer **Secrets**

When you combine real suede trim with the canvas, it gives the finished project a more upscale look. You can also use scraps of different colors of leather. Don't throw that old leather purse away! Recycle it into decorative trims.

Materials

- Lampshade (either round or square), any size
- Rectangular tray, any size
- Primed canvas (see Step 1 for the sizing)
- 3" x 9" piece of suede fabric
- Fabric glue
- Double-sided tape
- Acrylic paint*: 2 oz. Hauser green light
- 2" foam brush
- Scissors

* Used in this project: Plaid FolkArt Acrylic Paint

Lampshade

1 Cut one primed canvas strip 1½" wide by the circumference of a round lampshade or four times the length of one side of a square lampshade.

2 Paint the canvas strip with Hauser green light using the foam brush. Add a little water to the paint, just enough to make it the consistency of cream. Dip the foam brush into the paint and drag the brush down the canvas panel in a stria method, creating a pattern of fine, parallel lines (see page 12). Let dry.

3 Measure and mark the 1½" width of the canvas pieces on a scrap of suede. Within this width, draw some random animal stripes with a pencil. Refer to the pattern in the book or make up your own animal print design.

4 Cut out the suede designs using sharp scissors.

5 Use fabric glue to attach the suede pieces to the painted canvas strip and let dry.

6 Use double-sided tape to adhere the finished trim strip to the lampshade.

Designer **Secrets**

Using double-sided tape to temporarily apply decorative trim to accessories enables design changes. Consider painting the trim in teal and adding geometric designs in black or white for teen rooms. Or use any home décor stamp in a leaf motif for a garden room look.

Tray

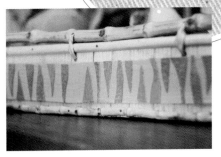

To make the tray, follow the instructions above, measuring the sides of the tray for length and width dimensions.

Tropical Leaf Decoration

When you can add dimension to a flat object, it seems to *come alive*. This project adds the unexpected decorating touch. You'll hear people say, "isn't that *clever!*" A combination of sprayed-on fabric dyes gives these leaves a surprisingly random look. No two look alike—just like in nature.

Materials

- Two 12" squares of primed canvas
- Tropical leaf pattern (see page 144)
- Transfer paper
- Pencil
- 9" of 18-gauge wire
- Wire cutters
- Color spray*: clover, lime and lemon peel
- Acrylic paint*: 2 oz. leaf green
- #6 round artist brush
- Scissors
- Sewing machine
- Covered surface

* Used in this project: Tulip Cool Color Spray, DecoArt Americana Acrylic Paint

1 On the primed side of the canvas, transfer the tropical leaf pattern using transfer paper and a pencil (see page 15). Flip the leaf pattern over and make a reverse transfer so that you have matching back-to-back leaves.

2 Cut out the leaves.

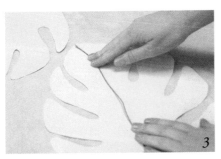

3 Use wire cutters to cut the length of the 22-gauge wire that will go up the center of the leaf, top to stem, approximately 8 to 9" per leaf.

4 Place the wire in center of the leaf, on the primed side of the canvas. Machine zigzag over the wire the length of the leaf.

Designer Secrets

- Make fall leaves using the same method. Just change the colors of the color spray to tangerine and coral red.
- The wire in the center of the leaf adds stability and lets you shape it into different configurations that stay put.
- A group of three leaves can add interest when loosely sculpted around a terra cotta pot with a potted plant.

5 Place the primed sides of the leaves together and machine zigzag with a close stitch around the entire outside edge of the new, complete leaf.

6 Place the leaf on a covered surface and spray it with combinations of the clover, lime and lemon peel color sprays, overlapping colors. Let one side dry and then repeat on the back side. You may want to repeat the process if you would like the leaf darker.

7 Use the #6 round artist brush dipped in leaf green acrylic paint to paint the center veins of the leaf.

Chapter (5)

Italian
Garden Kitchen

Picture yourself in an Italian villa as you head for your first cup of coffee in the morning. The Tuscan-inspired accessories in this kitchen will create that old-world *ambiance* in your own home.

Start with the crackle finish Vegetable Wall Plaques featuring originally designed artwork that you can copy and transfer onto canvas frames. The design of the overlapping Canvas Window Treatment can be adapted to easily fit just about any size window. The simple lines add *elegance* and allow light to filter through without obstructing the view. And because this window treatment is so classic, it can easily be customized to any décor by adding silk flowers or tassels. The highlight of this room is the fabulous Faux Tile Niche. Nothing says Italian better than *brightly* colored tile. This portable niche catches your eye the minute you see it, and it's such a snap to make using rub-ons. Complete the cozy look with the Decorative Chair Cover, delicately trimmed in gold. Transport your décor back in time with charming European style, creating your very own room with a view.

Vegetable and Fruit
Canvas Wall Plaques

Vegetables and fruits like grapes, artichokes and carrots
are some of the most *popular* motifs requested by
my clients for walls and accessories. These designs go in
just about every kitchen and breakfast area. The colors
chosen for the borders are Italian or Tuscan in flavor.
When the borders are painted in colors like lime, lavender
or teal, the motifs can take on a
contemporary flare.

Materials

- Heat transfer tool*
- Veggie and fruit designs (see pages 131-132)
- 2 each 11" and 2 each 13" wood frames (art supply stores)
- 4 pieces of 13" x 15" primed canvas
- Acrylic paints*: 2 oz. each antique gold, antique green and plum
- 2 oz. faux glazing medium*
- 3 foam brushes (1")
- Crackle base coat, large crackles*
- Crackle top coat*
- Medium oak stain*

- Cotton cloths or heavy-duty paper towels
- Staple gun and staples
- Painter's blue tape (1" wide)
- Paper or plastic plates
- Disposable latex gloves
- Measuring tape or ruler
- * Used in this project: Transfer Tool by Wall Lenk, DecoArt Faux Glazing Medium, Crafter's Pick Craqueleur Base Coat Large Crackles, Crafter's Pick Craqueleur Top Coat, Minwax Medium Oak Stain, DecoArt Americana Acrylic Paint

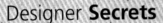

Designer **Secrets**

In this project, you don't need to be an artist because all of my artwork is reproduced and included in this book. Take the artwork to the copy center and have it photocopied. Then use the heat transfer tool to heat transfer the designs to the canvas. If you would like to purchase the artwork already printed on primed canvas, check the Resources for information (see page 130).

1 Cut out veggie and fruit designs (see pages 131-132) and make color copies at a copy center. Inkjet printers will not work with this technique.

2 Place the color copy face down onto one piece of primed canvas. Use the heat transfer tool to transfer the design (see page 14). Repeat this step for each design.

3 Mark a border around the images by measuring 1¾" from each edge of the canvas. Mask off the inside of the border with painter's blue tape. Paint the border and sides of the canvas panel using a foam brush with the following acrylic paint:

grapes and carrot ....antique gold
artichoke ....plum
beet ....antique green

4 Pour some crackle base coat onto a paper or plastic plate. Use a foam brush to apply a coat of the crackle base coat over the entire surface and sides of the canvas panels. Let dry. The surface will be clear, but slightly tacky.

5 Pour some crackle top coat onto a paper or plastic plate. Use a foam brush to apply a coat of crackle top coat over the entire surface and sides of the canvas panels. Let dry overnight. Cracks will appear when completely dry.

6 Add antiquing by applying a coat of medium oak stain over the surface with a heavy-duty paper towel or cotton cloth. Wipe off as much stain as desired with a clean, soft cotton cloth. Wear protective gloves and work in a well-ventilated area. Let dry.

7 Assemble the wood frames, following the manufacturer's instructions (or see page 19). The 11" pieces should be placed on the top and bottom; the 13" pieces will be the sides.

8 Stretch the canvas over the wood frames using the staple gun and staples (see page 20).

Faux Tile Niche

Hanging at the end of a long hallway, this faux tile niche creates a focal point that looks like it's actually built in. The project is a combination of faux painting to create dimension using shading and highlights and rub-on decorations. Its exotic appearance along with the portability and ease of installation makes it a *wonderful* addition to your décor.

Trompe l'oeil has become a very popular hand-painted request by homeowners in the past few years. Trompe l'oeil is the French expression that translates "fool or trick the eye." Anything that makes you wonder if it's real or not is considered trompe l'oeil. The Faux Tiled Niche is a wonderful "fool the eye" project. You do not need to be an artist to be able to create the project. With pretty rub-on designs, the niche becomes a faux tiled *accent* to any home. This niche looks so real, you might be tempted to place a vase with a single rose on the sill!

Materials

- 18" x 25" double primed canvas
- Acrylic Paints*: 2 oz. each honey brown, warm white, burnt umber, buttermilk, desert sand, toffee and blue/grey mist
- Rub-ons*: tuscan fruit
- Vinyl wallpaper paste, double-sided tape, or Velcro
- Paper or plastic plates
- 2 foam brushes (2")
- Artist liner brush
- Painter's blue tape (1" wide)

- Straight edge
- Measuring tape
- Pencil
- Scissors
- Craft stick or burnishing tool
- Paper towels

* Used for this project: Tulip Rub-On Transfer in MPD262 Tuscan Fruit, DecoArt Americana Acrylic Paint

Designer Secrets

The secret really is in the shadowing to create the trompe l'oeil look. Pay special attention to shadowing around the edges of the tiles, keeping in mind the direction of the light source. Heavier and lighter applications of shadowing allow for a more realistic look.

1 On the piece of 18" x 25" double primed canvas, make an arch shape at the top by measuring down from the top 5½" and drawing a horizontal line across the width of the canvas. Find the center of the canvas vertically and gently fold the canvas, matching the edges together at the horizontal line. Draw a curved line from the top center to the horizontal line at the edge. Cut through both thicknesses of canvas along the curved line. The arch will be symmetrical.

2 Mark a border around the niche by measuring 2½" in from each edge all the way around.

3

3

3 Using a straight edge and pencil, measure and mark four rows with three 4¼" square "tiles" inside the border of the niche. Leave ¼" between each "tile" for grout lines. The area at the top of the curved arch will not be divided into "tiles."

4

4 Pour some buttermilk acrylic paint onto a paper or plastic plate. Paint the inside tile squares using a foam brush.

5

5 Use painter's blue tape to mask off the border by placing the tape on the inside mark of the border. Use short strips of tape to go around the arched top, placing the strips at angles to preserve the rounded curve. Burnish the edges of the tape with the craft stick or burnishing tool so the paint will not seep underneath.

6 Pour small amounts of honey brown, warm white, burnt umber and buttermilk paint onto a paper or plastic plate. Using a foam brush, pick up the buttermilk and burnt umber paints, mixing them slightly. Paint the border area, dragging the foam brush up the taped area.

7 Use burnt umber paint with a clean foam brush to shade the edges where shadows might be darker and where the ledge joins the walls of the niche. Miter the corners at the lower left and right to create the look of a ledge. Consider the location of the light source and how shadows would naturally be cast. For example, in my niche, I viewed the light source as coming from the upper left, so the right side border will show more light than the left border. Pick up warm white on a foam brush to add highlights to the right border and the center of the ledge. Let dry. Remove the tape.

8 Use a clean foam brush to individually paint tiles with desert sand, being sure not to paint the grout lines. A free-form feeling along the lines is preferable for a softer look. If you feel more comfortable, tape off each tile. Let dry.

9 Dip the foam brush into the toffee paint and dry brush onto paper towels. Use it to apply shadows along the inside edges of the tiles.

10 Cut apart the rub-on designs. Following the manufacturer's instructions, burnish the designs onto the tiles using a craft stick or burnishing tool.

11 Lift up the Mylar and smooth the design with your hand.

12 Dip an artist liner brush into blue/grey mist paint mixed with a little water. Paint the grout lines. Let dry. Clean the artist liner brush. Dip it into warm white acrylic paint to add highlights to the grout lines.

13 To install the Faux Tile Niche, use vinyl wallpaper paste, double-sided tape or Velcro to adhere the canvas to the wall. Follow the manufacturer's instructions if you choose to use vinyl wallpaper paste.

Canvas Window Treatment

Simple, yet *classic* in design, this window treatment lends itself to numerous decorative treatments and themes. By adding braided cording and a tassel, the window treatment can fit into a *traditional* home. By adding dried vines, silk leaves and grapes, the window takes on the look of an Italian villa.

Materials

- Canvas fabric (see Step 1 for sizing)
- Canvas window treatment basic shape (see page 136 and englarge according to the instructions on page 21)
- Wood closet pole to fit the length of your window as a drapery rod
- Staple gun and staples
- Sewing machine
- Measuring tape

Note: Measurements are given for sample purposes only. Be sure to measure your window for accurate measurements. The proportion of the layered panels is the most important part.

Designer **Secrets**

Closet poles and wood finials are reasonably priced and found in home improvement centers. They are easy to paint, stain or faux finish to match any room's wall paint, décor or window treatment.

1 To make the large base panel, measure the width of the window. Divide the width in half. This will be the finished width of each of the two larger panels. Add 1" to this measurement and cut two rectangles 22" long by the new width. On one long edge, find the center and mark. On each edge, measure up 5" from the long edge and mark. Connect the center marks with the marks on the edges. Cut along the lines. The fabric panels will be "house" shaped (see the basic shape on page 136). Each large panel is a double thickness, so cut two "house" shaped pieces for each panel. Cut two panels (a total of four pieces of fabric). For example, for a 48" window, make two large panels (4 pieces) each size 25" wide x 22" long (at the longest point).

2 Place right sides together and machine stitch around three sides, leaving the long edge open. Turn right-side out and press flat. Top stitch across the top opening ¼" from the edge.

3 For the second layer, make two panels approximately 5" narrower than the finished size of the base panels by 15" long at the point. The measurements are for the finished panels, so add 1" to both the height and width when cutting the panels. For example, for the same 48" window, the measurement would be 20" x 16". Follow the instructions above for construction.

4 Make one small panel approximately 9" wide x 12" long at the longest point. Sew it together the same way (see Step 2).

Installation

1 Cut a closet pole or dowel the desired width of the window. Finish or paint as desired. Find the center of the pole. Mark with a pencil. Staple one large panel to the left and one panel to the right of the center mark. Staple the panels evenly through the fabric into the pole.

3 Overlay the smaller panel directly over the center of the pole between the other two panels. Staple in place.

2 Overlay the second layer panels onto the first, centering them on top of the base panels. Staple in place along the pole, being careful not to staple directly over the previously inserted staples.

Use your creativity with the Canvas Window Treatment. The addition of *tassels*, *vines* or additional *fabrics* can dramatically change the look of your window.

Canvas **Chair Cover**

Re-covering chair seats can be time consuming, especially when you have six to eight chairs to re-cover. These *easy-to-make* canvas chair covers can be made in an afternoon. They store flat so they take up very little space. They can also be made in a variety of themes and colors for the holidays. Think of how much fun it would be to make blank chair covers for a special occasion, like a family reunion, special anniversary or birthday. Each guest could sign his or her chair seat with a special message using a fabric marking pen. The chair seats could become "chair autograph covers" for years of *special occasions*.

Note: Materials and instructions are for one chair.

Materials

- Straight back chair with upholstered or wood seat
- Unprimed canvas (see Step 1 for sizing)
- 2 yd. ribbon (2" wide)
- Decorative trim, quantity is the perimeter of the chair seat
- 4 metal charms
- Scissors or rotary cutter and mat
- Sewing machine

Designer **Secrets**

- There is no need to hem the panel edges. If you are worried about the canvas unraveling, apply fabric fray stop liquid product to the cut edges before sewing on the trim.
- Fabric panels are a quick and inexpensive way to change the look of your chairs. If your chair has a hard surface for a seat, place foam, a purchased chair cover or folded quilt batting on the chair seat first, then tie the canvas chair cover onto the seat. It will add instant comfort and instant style at the same time.

1 Measure the length and width of the chair seat. It is not necessary to remove the seats from the chairs.

2 Cut canvas fabric 3" larger than the chair seat all the way around.

3 Cut four 18" pieces of the ribbon. Fold each ribbon in the center, twist it, and then stitch one ribbon to each corner of the seat panel.

4 Flip the panel over so that the sewn ribbon is on the backside. Sew the trim all around the panel.

5 Hand sew a charm onto each corner.

6 Attach the covers to the chair seat by tying the ribbon around the chair legs.

Crackled Canvas
Flower and Bird Design

When I showed my husband, David, this finished project, I did not tell him I had made it. He thought I'd found the *framed art* at an antique shop and it had cost a bundle! Oh, the money I save making my own home décor and craft projects!

Materials

- Heat transfer tool*
- Frame
- Artwork to fit in your frame
- Lightweight canvas fabric (see Step 1 for sizing)
- Small round artist brush
- Crackle base coat, large cracks*
- Crackle top coat*
- Mounting glue*
- Gold rub-on paint*
- Medium oak stain*
- Matte board or foam core
- Paper or plastic plates

- 3 foam brushes (2")
- Scissors
- Ruler
- Cotton cloth
- Iron
- Disposable latex gloves
- Wax paper
- Heavy book
- * Used in this project: Transfer Tool by Wall Lenk, Crafter's Pick Craqueleur Large Cracks, Crafter's Pick Craqueleur Top Coat, Crafter's Pick Mounting Glue, Minwax Wood Stain, Rub 'n' Buff Rub-On Paint

Designer Secrets

I found that you can add accents of color to the canvas-transferred images using acrylic paints mixed with glazing mediums. I mix ⅓ paint to ⅔ glaze. Pour small amounts of coordinating acrylic paints onto a palette, then pour some glazing medium onto the palette. Dip an artist brush into the glazing medium and small amount of paint. Blend on the palette. Lightly brush the color on the canvas on any area you wish to bring out more design color. Let dry.

1 Measure the inside of the frame. Cut a piece of canvas 2" larger than the frame measurement all the way around. Iron out any wrinkles.

2 Make a color copy of the artwork you've chosen. Cut the artwork apart and determine the placement on the canvas. Place the color copy face down on the canvas. Use the heat transfer tool to transfer the design (see page 14). The transferred design will be lighter than the original and more antique in appearance.

3 Measure the inside dimensions of the frame and cut matte board or foam core according to those measurements. Use a foam brush to apply mounting glue to the matte board or foam core.

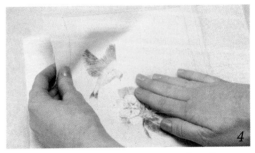

4 Adhere the canvas to the matte board or foam core, smoothing out the wrinkles with your hands. Wrap the canvas to the back side of the board and glue with the mounting glue. Place a piece of wax paper and a heavy book over the front and let dry overnight.

5 Use a foam brush to apply the crackle base coat to the front of the canvas. Let dry. The glue will be clear, but slightly tacky.

6 Use a foam brush to apply the crackle top coat over the top of the front of the canvas. Cracks will appear when dry.

7 Wear latex gloves and use a cotton cloth to apply the oak stain and antique. Wipe off as much stain as desired with paper towels or a cotton cloth, leaving the excess stain in the cracks to simulate an antique effect.

8 The frame can be crackled and antiqued using the same techniques. Rub accents of gold paint onto the frame.

9 Mount the canvas image in the frame when complete.

Chapter (6)

Outdoor **Living**

You'll be dining al fresco when you turn your drab backyard into an *outdoor oasis*. Enclose a tent-style canopy with Canvas Canopy Side Panels designed with window cut-outs that add intimacy and privacy, but allow the breeze to keep you cool. Lighten up the outdoor room with garden-style Tomato Cage Garden Accent Lights. Cover the tomato cage frame with stenciled canvas, place it over a dowel wrapped with holiday mini-lights, and watch your guests' faces glow.

Speaking of holiday lights, the next project adds *sparkle* and mood. The Canvas Trapezoid Light Covers look like tiny lampshades that fit over each mini-light. You won't be able to wait until nightfall to turn them on. On the floor, place the Patio Floorcloth. Complete with a pond and stepping stones, it's a great conversation piece at a party and will have your guests asking if they can feed the fish.

Dine in *comfort* in the Easy Patio Stenciled Director's Chairs. Everyone will also get a kick out of the Stenciled Stepping Stone Placemats.

Canvas Canopy **Side Panels**

Canvas panels are the perfect way to add privacy or protection from the elements, day or night, and make a great outdoor *entertaining* area. Decorate them with stencils or stamps to go with your *garden theme*. The canvas window flap can be removed instead of rolling it up and tying, which adds versatility. If you live in a windy area, secure the sides of the canvas panels to the metal frame with strips of hook-and-loop tape.

Materials

- Purchased metal frame canopy
- 3 panels wide of heavy canvas (72" wide x the length of your canopy)
- Nylon window screen on a roll (36" wide)
- Hook-and-loop tape with sticky back
- 1½ yd. nylon cording (⅜" wide)
- Fabric adhesive*
- Straight pins
- Measuring tape
- Pencil
- Scissors or rotary cutter and mat
- Sewing machine and matching thread
- Iron
- * Used in this project: Aleene's Platinum Bond Super Fabric Textile Adhesive

Designer **Secrets**

When working with canvas, use a glue that is super strong, dries clear and is washable.

1 Determine the width and length for the side panels of the canopy. Measure the height of your canopy for the length of your panel. Determine how many panels you will need on each side. My canopy frame was 73" wide, so I just used one 72" wide panel and measured the length for each of my side panels. My panels were cut 95" long and had a 4" bottom hem and 4" rod pocket. I added 1" to turn under ½" seam allowances at the top and bottom. The total cut piece was 104" long. Depending on the opening of each side of the canopy, you may have one panel or two panels. You may choose to make two panels on one side to create a "doorway" for easier access and keep the other three side panels as single panels.

2 There's no need to hem the sides of the fabric panel if it fits the width of the opening. If you use more than one panel per side, be sure to add a 1" seam allowance for each side. Double turn under ½", press, and machine stitch.

3 Make a rod pocket deep enough to accommodate the metal rod of your canopy design. Turn under the top of the curtain along the top fold line for its finished edge, then turn under the cut edge ½". Press and pin in place. Topstitch through all layers along the inner fold line at the lower edge of the rod pocket.

4 Turn the bottom hem up, fold under the raw edge, and machine stitch or glue with the fabric adhesive.

5 Decide on the size you would like for the window screen opening of your panel. My window screen is 45" wide x 30" high. Measure and center the placement of the window opening on the panel.

Tip Cut a mock screen window template out of craft paper if you are unsure of the size and placement.

6 Measure and mark the placement of the screen on the side panel with a pencil. Cut out using sharp scissors.

7 Cut window screen material 2" wider and higher than the opening. Pin or use tape to secure it in place, centered in the opening. Machine stitch around all edges. Trim excess screen using scissors. My measurements were 49" wide x 34" high.

Note I found that canvas does not have a right or wrong side, unlike other fabrics. Choose a side you wish to be the inside of the canopy panel.

8 Make "bias tape" canvas pieces to frame the screen window. Cut strips 1½" x the length of the window. (For example, since my measurements were 49" wide by 34" high, I doubled the length and width for a total of 166".) Fold them in half in the center, then fold each edge into the center fold and press. Either machine stitch down the center or use fabric glue. If using fabric glue, allow to dry overnight. Cover each edge with bias tape canvas pieces.

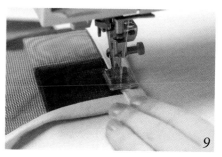

9 Canvas bias tape pieces are made for both sides of the window screen opening. Sandwich the screen between the folds of the bias tape, then stitch along the edge. Slightly overlap where corners meet. Trim off any excess in lengths. Pin or tape in place. Machine stitch or use the fabric adhesive to attach. If using the fabric adhesive, place a board and heavy objects on top of the glued pieces to dry flat overnight.

10 To make the window flap, measure the screen opening. Cut a canvas panel 3" wider and 3" longer than the opening to make a window flap. (Since my window opening measured 45" wide by 30" high, my flap measured 48" x 33".) Press ¼" hem all around the flap panel. Machine stitch or use the fabric adhesive to secure the hem.

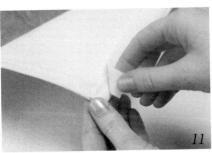

11 Attach one side of a length of hook-and-loop tape to the top edge of the canvas window flap.

12 Attach the other side of the hook-and-loop tape to the top of the screen window on the inside of the panel. Before pressing both sides of the hook-and-loop tape together, place a length of cording 18" long on the left and right sides of the hook-and-loop tape. This cording will be used to tie up the canvas flap when it is rolled up.

Tomato Cage Garden
Accent Light

How does one come up with the idea of using a wire tomato cage to make an *outdoor light?* Well, take a couple of good friends tossing ideas back and forth, throw in a little talk about an exciting, new, fresh tomato sauce, and the next thing you know, you're lighting a tomato cage! This project adds a decorative touch indoors or outdoors on a sunny day, but when the sun goes down, the Tomato Cage Light adds a *warm glow* of filtered light through the canvas. Add silk plants or the Canvas Plant project found in Chapter 4.

Materials

- 4-foot metal cone-shaped tomato cage
- 2 yd. unprimed canvas (48" wide)
- 14" to 16" diameter plant container
- Plastic liner for plants
- Styrofoam
- 1 strand white holiday mini-lights
- 3-foot wooden dowel (1" in diameter)
- Mylar
- Disappearing fabric marker
- Fabric glue or glue gun and hot glue
- Acrylic paint*: 2 oz. each light avocado, light sage and mink tan
- Bamboo pattern (see page 137)
- Double ended stencil brush*
- Paper or plastic plate
- Paper towels
- Scissors
- Craft knife or electric stencil cutting pen
- Painter's blue tape (1" wide)
- Sewing machine and matching thread
- * Used in this project: Stencil Ease Double Ended Stencil Brush, DecoArt Americana Acrylic Paint

Designer **Secrets**

Hold the glued canvas in place at the top of the tomato cage with clothespins until dry. If necessary, trim the length of the metal prongs of the tomato cage to shorten it slightly. An uplight could also be used in place of the mini-lights and wooden dowel.

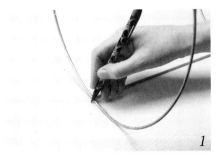

1 To make the pattern for the canvas cover, place the tomato cage on a piece of canvas. Place a piece of painter's blue tape next to one of the vertical prongs of the tomato cage to designate the beginning point. Holding a disappearing fabric marker or pencil at the top edge of the cage, begin carefully rolling the cage on the canvas, keeping the marker point on the canvas so that it makes a continuous line as the cage rolls. Keep rolling until you reach the beginning point.

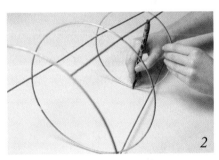

2 Return the cage to the original point and repeat Step 1, drawing the line at the bottom of the third metal frame of the cone shape. Draw two straight lines to connect the top and bottom lines at the side edges.

3 Add ¾" to the top, bottom, and sides for seam and hem allowances. Cut out the canvas on the outer markings.

4 Using the bamboo pattern, Mylar and the craft knife or the electric stencil cutting pen, cut out your own bamboo stencil (see page 16).

5 Lay the canvas cover flat on a surface. Place the newly cut stencil on the canvas. Pour a small amount of light avocado and mink tan paint onto a paper or plastic plate.

6 Dip a stencil brush into the light avocado and remove the excess by wiping it onto paper towels. Using a swirling motion, apply the paint over the bamboo stencil.

7 Use separate stencil brushes to apply highlights of light sage and mink tan. Since the dry brush technique is used when stenciling the acrylic paint, it is quickly dry enough to stencil over. Lift up the stencil to check your progress.

8 Lift up the stencil and reposition it on another part of the canvas pattern. Repeat the stenciling process. Let the paint dry completely. Remember that you can flip the stencil over to reverse the design. Be sure to wipe off any wet paint on the stencil before reversing.

9 Wrap the canvas around the tomato cage to check for fit. Make any adjustments on the side seam by marking them with a disappearing fabric marker on the wrong side of the canvas. The finished piece should fit nicely, but not tightly.

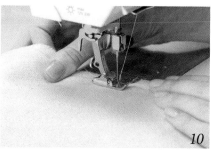

10 With right sides together, sew up the side seam. Press the seam open. Turn under a double 1¼" hem on the bottom of the canvas. Press and sew the hem in place. Turn the canvas cover right-side out. The top edge will be unfinished.

11 Place the tomato cage on a tabletop with the large round end down. Slip the canvas over, stenciled side out.

12 Flip the tomato cage up so you can fold over the top hem onto the frame. Wrap the canvas around the top of the tomato cage and use fabric glue or hot glue to secure.

13 Wrap a wood dowel with one strand of white holiday mini-lights.

15 Push the metal prongs of the tomato cage into the Styrofoam, over the wooden dowel. Plug in the lights.

14 Place the plastic liner into the plant container. Wedge pieces of Styrofoam into the plant container. Push the dowel wrapped in lights into the Styrofoam.

Patio **Floorcloth**

I am so amused whenever I place this floorcloth on the floor. People will walk on it but "step over" the *pond* as if they were going to get their feet wet! We are such creatures of habit! And speaking of creatures, it really is the finishing touches of the creatures in the pond and on the stepping stones that give the *whimsical* life to the floorcloth.

Designer **Secrets**

• I recommend double primed canvas #10 for this project because of its weight and also because there is no need to hem the edges. If you cannot find this product, then add extra coats of gesso or acrylic primer to the back of the product you purchased.

• I use discarded foam containers as paint palettes. They work perfectly because of the raised sides. After use, just toss them out.

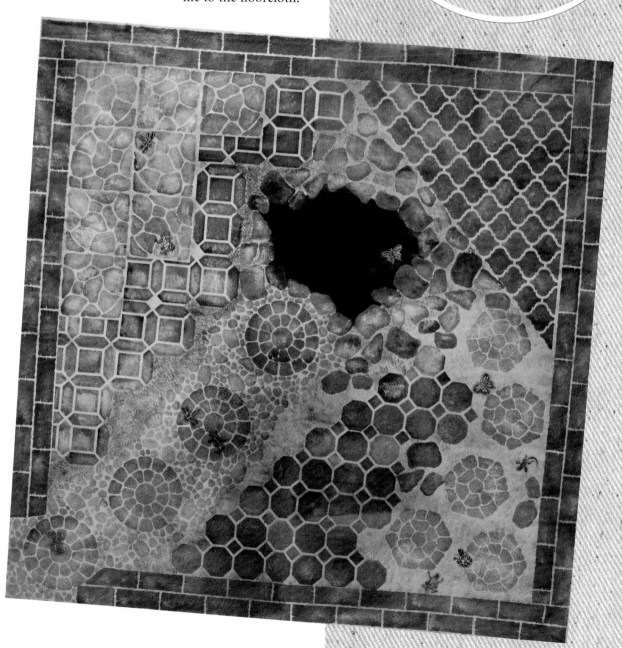

Materials

- 2 pieces double primed canvas, 3 yd. x 54"
- Stencils*: straight brick, river rock, Italian tile, Spanish tile, small flagstones, Mexican pavers, 11" square stepping stone, 14" round stepping stone, 12" hexagon stepping stone, frog, lizard, butterfly
- 1 qt. cream-colored wall paint with a low sheen
- Foam roller
- Paint tray and plastic liner
- Patio paint*: 2 oz. each patio brick, concrete grey, antique mum, terra cotta, honey brown, tango blue, cloud white, golden honey, light sage green, chive green, pinecone brown, hydrangea blue, pansy purple and fuchsia

- Natural sea sponge
- 3 stencil brushes (½")
- Palette
- 3 foam brushes (2")
- Plastic bucket or container
- Painter's blue tape (1" wide)
- Heavy-duty duct tape (3" wide)
- Clear acrylic sealer
- Pencil
- * Used in this project: DecoArt Patio Paint, StenSource Stencils: Straight Brick W5701, River Rock W5702, Italian Tile W5703, Spanish Tile W5704, Small Flagstones W5706, Mexican Pavers W5707, 11" Square BD5702, 14" Round BD5703, 12" Hexagon BD5704, 7" Garden Friends 1 BD9007

1 The two lengths of canvas will be joined together in the center to make a square floorcloth approximately 9 feet x 9 feet. Place the canvas on a large, flat, covered surface (a garage floor would work) and tape the panels together in the center using heavy-duty duct tape. After taping, place the taped side down.

2 The canvas is double primed, however, it still needs a coat of paint so that the background is not so white. Use any brand of interior wall paint in a low sheen cream color. Low sheen means that the finish on the paint is not flat, nor is it semigloss or gloss paint. You might have leftover interior paint from your home that would work well. Pour the cream-colored wall paint into a paint tray lined with a plastic liner. Roll on an even coat of paint onto the floorcloth using a foam roller. Let dry. Clean the roller.

3 At this point, you may choose to use a pencil and lightly mark the placement of the stepping stone path and pond. Remember, there is no right or wrong way to complete this project. Whatever leftover areas you have can be filled in with small flagstones, river rock, or sponged grass.

Border

1 First, use the straight brick stencil as a border around the outside of the floorcloth. Notice that on the opposite side of the floorcloth, the brick is stenciled end-to-end. On the other two sides, the brick is stenciled within the remaining area with the exception of one corner where the brick border is left open enough to fit the 14" round stepping stone and path in the pond area.

2 Place the brick stencil on one corner. If you wish, use painter's blue tape to tape off any adjoining brick area of the stencil that you do not wish to paint. Pour some patio brick, concrete grey, and antique mum paint onto a large palette. Dip a sea sponge into a plastic container of water and wring it out. Dip the sea sponge into the patio brick paint and dab it onto the brick stencil. Pick up some concrete grey and antique mum on the sea sponge and lightly dab onto the brick stencil to create a more brick-like look and definition.

3 Lift up the stencil. Let the first area dry a little before placing the stencil down again next to the first section. At this time, you may wish to work back and forth on opposite sides of the floorcloth border so the paint has a chance to dry. Rinse out the sea sponge in water at any time that it becomes too muddy with paint colors or use several sea sponges to apply the various paint colors.

4   When you have finished two sides of the border, place the stencil on the corner and continue to finish the brick border on all sides, leaving an opening for the path. Let dry.

Details

1   Refer to the photo for the placement of the tiles, stepping stones, path and stone-lined pond.

2   Place the Spanish tile stencil in one corner of the floorcloth. Use painter's blue tape to tape off the edge where the Spanish tile stencil will meet the brick border. Use a clean sea sponge to sponge this area using the terra cotta and honey brown paint.

3   Place the 11" square stepping stone stencil in the adjacent corner of the floorcloth. Use painter's blue tape to tape off the edge where the 11" square stepping stone stencil will meet the brick border. Use a clean sea sponge to sponge this area with combinations of antique mum, golden honey and pinecone brown paint.

4   Sponge the opposite corner in the same way and with the same colors as Step 11, but use the 12" hexagon stencil.

5   Sponge the path using the 14" round stepping stone and antique mum, concrete grey and honey brown. Dip the sponge in the colors without cleaning betwen colors to create a mix of colors.

6   Place the round stepping stone stencil on a piece of craft paper or open paper bag. Draw around the outside of the stones to make a paper pattern. Cut out with scissors. It does not need to be perfect—just a 14" circle to place onto the painted stepping stone to protect it from getting paint on it while sponging the next step.

7   Use the river rock stencil to lightly sponge around the round stepping stone pathway. Sponge using cloud white, concrete grey and antique mum paint.

8   Use a cleaned dampened sea sponge to sponge light sage green around the stepping stones (see the photo for placement). Lightly sponge this color onto a stepping stone to give it a mossy look.

9 Sponge the Italian tile stencil with combinations of patio brick, pinecone brown and concrete grey paint (see the photo for placement).

10 Sponge the Mexican pavers with combinations of hydrangea blue and cloud white (see the photo for placement).

11 Use the small flagstone stencil to sponge an irregular shaped circle of stones lining the outside of the pond. Sponge the stones with pinecone brown, antique mum and light sage green paints (see the photo for placement).

12 Pour some hydrangea blue and tango blue paint onto a palette. Use a foam brush dipped into tango blue to paint around the stones.

13 As you paint into the center of the pond, use mixtures of the two blue colors so that the pond becomes lighter in the center area and darker around the stones.

14 Use a slightly dampened sea sponge to sponge light sage green and chive green around the pond stones.

Finishing Touches

1 Stencil a butterfly on the pond by first stenciling the butterfly in cloud white. Let dry. Reposition the stencil over the top and stencil the wings in fuchia and pansy purple. Stencil the body in concrete grey. Using the same method, stencil the frogs, lizards and butterflies on the stepping stones in the colors of your choice.

2 Apply two to three coats of clear acrylic sealer to the floorcloth using a foam roller. Let dry between coats.

Canvas Trapezoid **Light Covers**

"Aren't these adorable ... and they add such *fun* to a plain strand of mini-lights!" That's what my photo stylist, Kim, exclaimed when she saw this project.

The sun was setting as we were patiently awaiting dusk and the final photograph of the day. It was amazing that as long of a day as it had been, the mini-lights seemed to *brighten* the end just right.

This project is a great one for a group to get together and create an assembly line of light covers! Wait for an event at dusk when you can use twinkling mini-lights as stars.

Designer **Secrets**

Use a clothespin to secure the glued edge until the glue gets tacky. Use a multi-colored strand of lights, but insert white lights wherever a trapezoid light cover is located.

Materials

- 2 yd. primed canvas
- Trapezoid pattern (see page 137)
- Copper leafing pen*
- Gold leafing pen*
- Fabric glue or double-sided tape (¼" wide)
- Strand of holiday mini-lights

- Scissors
- Kitchen knife
- Straight edge
- Pencil

* Used in this project: Krylon Copper Leafing Pen, Krylon 18K Gold Leafing Pen

1 Trace around the trapezoid pattern onto the primed canvas with a pencil.

2 Cut out the canvas.

3 Draw a border around the bottom edge of the unprimed side of the trapezoid using the copper leafing pen. Let dry.

4 Draw a border line just above the copper line using the gold leafing pen.

5 Fold in the ¼" flap for the seam and crease using scissors or the dull side of a knife.

6 Crease all of the fold lines using scissors or the dull side of a knife, following the pattern.

7 Use the fabric glue or double-sided tape to attach the seam to the inside of the lampshade.

8 Push the light covers onto the mini-lights from underneath. They will hang above the light bulbs.

Stepping Stone Placemats

I've sponged and stenciled concrete stepping stones for years. I've even created *faux* stepping stones on concrete patios. It didn't occur to me to make a stepping stone placemat until one day when I was *stenciling* a patio long past noon and my stomach started singing a lunch tune. My thoughts turned to dining on a stepping stone placemat. Doesn't everything revolve around food! Note: Materials and instructions are for four placemats.

Designer Secrets

To keep the stenciled placemat from curling up, paint the back side of the canvas with a coat of acrylic paint.

Materials

- 1 yd. double sided primed canvas
- Stencils*: 14" round stepping stone, frog, turtle
- Patio paint*: 2 oz. each antique mum, golden honey, sage green, pinecone brown, wrought iron black, mistletoe green, sprout green, terra cotta and cloud white
- Sea sponge
- 2" foam brush
- 3 stencil brushes (½")

- Paper or plastic plates
- Painter's blue tape (1" wide)
- Paper towels
- Lampshade or large plate (14" in diameter)
- Pencil
- * Used in this project: StenSource Stencils: 14" Round BD5703, 7" Garden Friend 2 BD9008, DecoArt Patio Paint

1 Use the lampshade or large plate to trace 14" circles on the canvas. Cut out the circles.

Tip Stencil the stepping stone stencil on a 14½" square of canvas and cut away the excess around the stone. This is an easy way to be accurate!

2 Paint the canvas rounds with a base coat of antique mum acrylic paint using a foam brush. Allow to dry.

3 Place the stepping stone stencil onto the canvas round. Tape it in place using painter's blue tape.

4 Pour small amounts of pinecone brown, golden honey and antique mum paint onto a paper or plastic plate. Use a dampened sea sponge to randomly sponge the colors onto the stencil. Mix the colors on the stone areas. Remove the stencil and allow to dry.

Colors for the Frog

1 Align the frog body stencil onto the canvas placemat and tape it in place. Pour a small amount of mistletoe green paint onto a paper or plastic plate. Dip a stencil brush into the paint and dab onto paper towels to remove the excess paint. Stipple the paint over the stencil body (see page 18).

2 Align the frog "spots and face" stencil. Use a stencil brush to apply sprout green and highlights of pinecone brown and cloud white.

3 Lift up the stencil. Allow to dry.

Colors for the Turtle

1 Align the turtle body stencil onto the canvas placemat and tape it in place. Pour a small amount of antique mum acrylic paint onto a paper or plastic plate. Dip the stencil brush into the paint and dab it onto the stencil. Add deeper accents of wrought iron black around the outside edges of the turtle. Remove the stencil and let dry.

2 Align the turtle "spots and face" stencil. Use a stencil brush to apply sprout green with highlights of cloud white paint on the turtle's shell.

3 Lift up the stencil. Allow to dry.

Easy Patio Stenciled
Director's Chairs

Stenciling director's chairs is one of the easiest ways to add *character* to a blank canvas seat and back. And who would guess that you can use floor stencils on a chair! These chairs are also fun stenciled in geometric designs for teen rooms or in a lodge look for a casual *outdoor porch*. I found that my guests always seek out their favorite frog or bee chair when they come for a visit.

Materials

- Director's chair frame
- 1 yd. unprimed canvas for each chair or purchased canvas chair covers
- Stencils*: Frog, bee, flower pot
- 3 stencil brushes (½")
- Acrylic paints*: 2 oz. each wash white, marigold, raw sienna, Hauser green light, Hauser green dark, sapphire, Paynes gray, pansy lavendar, red violet, petal pink and black

- Painter's blue tape (1" wide)
- Paper or plastic plates
- Paper towels
- Scissors
- Iron
- Measuring tape
- Sewing machine
- Permanent black marking pen (fine)
- * Used in this project: DecoArt Americana Acrylic Paint, StenSource Stencils: Flower pot and Bee BD5708, 12" Frog BD5715

Designer **Secrets**

- When stenciling on colored canvas, the colors will be more true to the paint color if you first stencil the entire area lightly in white. The layered paint colors will then pop with their true color.
- Remember you can use a stencil brush in another color before cleaning if the next color you use is in the same family. For example, start stenciling light greens, then medium greens and finally dark greens. You can even go to burnt umber after the dark green as long as you stay in the darker family. Dry brushing by removing most of the paint color onto paper towels until you barely see any paint on the brush will also ensure that the next paint color used will not be affected by the previous paint color.

Chair Back

1 Determine the width of the chair back from side to side and front to back.

2 For the length, add 1" to the measurement at the top and bottom for hems. For the width, add 4" to each side to create pockets.

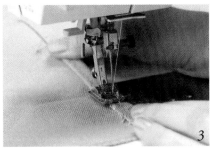

3 Press under 1" along the top and bottom edges, then fold ½" to the inside to create a ½" hem. Topstitch close to the folded edge.

4 Press 4" under on each end. Turn under ½" and topstitch close to the folded edge.

Chair Seat

1 Determine the width of the chair seat from side to side and front to back.

2 For the length, add 1" to the front and back of the seat measurement. For the width, add 1½" to each side to create pockets.

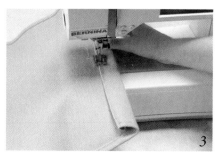

3   Press under 1" along the front and back edge of chair seat, then fold ½" to the inside to create a ½" hem. Topstitch close to the folded edge.

4   Press under 1½" on each side. Turn under ½" seam and topstitch close to the folded edge.

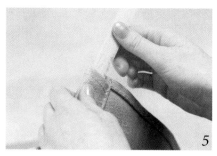

5   Slide the wooden dowel chair frame inside each side pocket.

Stenciling

(For stenciling instructions, see page 18.)

Bee

1   Tape off any area of the stencil you do not wish to get paint into using painter's blue tape.

2   Stencil the wings and body first with wash white acrylic paint. Let dry.

3   Add marigold acrylic paint to the body and edges of the wings. Add wash white highlights on the wings.

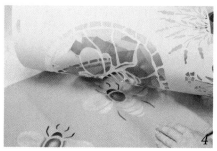

4   Stencil the antennas, legs and middle section of the head of the bee with black. Use a clean stencil brush to add a small amount of wash white to the middle of the bee. Remove the stencil.

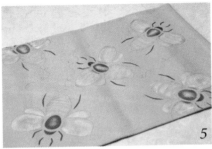

5 Draw squiggle loops with the fine line permanent black marking pen.

Flower pot

1 Stencil the back of the chair with the flower pot using raw sienna. Highlight it with wash white. Stencil the flowers using pansy lavender and petal pink. Stencil the leaves using combinations of Hauser green light and Hauser green dark.

2 Loosely outline the flowers and leaves with the fine line permanent black marking pen.

Frog

1 Stencil the frog using Hauser green dark first. With a clean stencil brush, add red violet highlights over the green.

Stepping stones

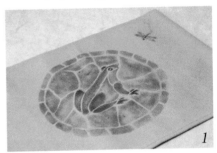

1 Stencil the stones using raw sienna, Paynes gray and small amounts of Hauser green light and red violet. Stencil the colors randomly, mixing them on the stone.

Dragonfly

1 Stencil the back of the chair with the dragonfly using black for the legs, wash white for the wings and red violet as an accent on the wings.

Garden **Apron**

I couldn't resist painting this apron with
the same stone and frog motifs that I used
on the placemats! It became the perfect gift
for a friend who is an avid
green-thumb gardener.

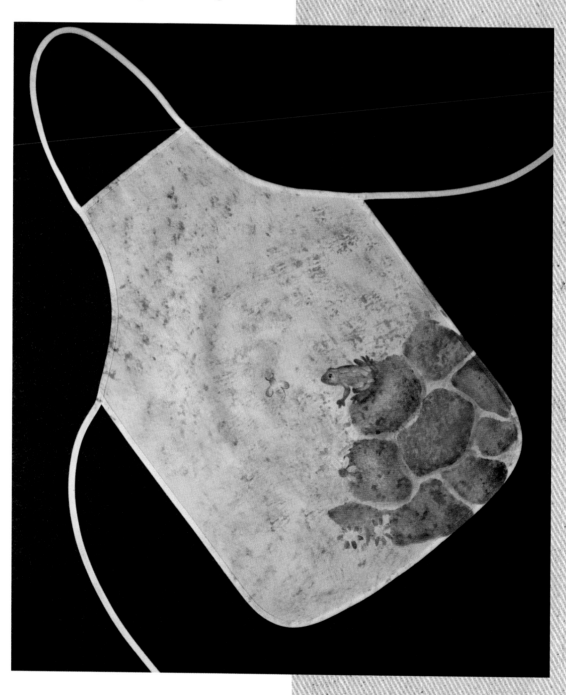

Materials

- Canvas apron
- Stencils*: 14" round stepping stone, frog, dragonfly
- Brushable fabric paint*: 1 oz each linen, golden tan, lime, chocolate, ebony, olive, holiday green and periwinkle
- Natural sea sponge
- 3 stencil brushes (½")
- Paper or plastic plates

- Painter's blue tape (1" wide)
- Paper towels
- Iron
- Covered work surface
- * Used in this project: Tulip Soft Brushable Fabric Paint, StenSource Stencils: Garden Friends 4 BD9010, 14" Round BD5701

Designer **Secrets**

I remember the days before fabric paint when I mixed textile medium with acrylic paint to make the paint softer. While that still works, using a product that is especially made for fabric is so much easier and keeps the painted apron soft, yet it can be machine washed.

1 Purchase a canvas apron of your choice at a craft store. Pre-wash, dry and iron it flat. Place the apron on a covered work surface.

2 Dip a sea sponge into water and wring it out completely. Pour some olive and lime paint onto a paper or plastic plate. Dip the sea sponge into both colors and randomly and lightly sponge them over the entire apron.

3 Place the stepping stone stencil onto the apron. Decide which stones you wish to sponge and where the placement of stones will be on the apron. Use painter's blue tape to tape over any adjacent stones you do not wish to sponge.

4 Pour small amounts of chocolate, golden tan, olive, lime and linen paint onto a paper or plastic plate. Use a dampened sea sponge to randomly sponge the colors onto the stones, mixing the colors on the stone areas. Remove the stencil and allow the paint to dry.

5 Align the frog body stencil onto one of the stones on the apron. Tape the stencil in place. Pour a small amount of holiday green onto a paper or plastic plate. Dip a stencil brush into the paint and dab it onto paper towels to remove the excess paint. Swirl the paint over the frog body.

6 Align the frog "spots and face" stencil. Use a clean stencil brush to apply lime paint. Highlight with chocolate and linen paint using a clean stencil brush.

7 Stencil the dragonfly using black on the antenna and legs, periwinkle on the wings and lime on the body, using a clean stencil brush when applying the colors.

Stepping Stone
Floorcloth

This small and *less complicated* version of the patio floorcloth is often requested as a housewarming gift for an avid gardener. Using the same materials and techniques to sponge and stencil, you will be able to create this floorcloth quickly and receive rave reviews!

Materials

- 2 foot x 3 foot double primed canvas
- Stencils*: 14" round stepping stone, lizard, frog, ivy
- Acrylic paint*: 2 oz. each caramel, charcoal, light parchment, neutral grey, celery green, avocado, black, wash white and raw umber
- Natural sea sponge
- 3 stencil brushes (½")
- Mini foam roller

- Paint tray
- Paper or plastic plates
- Paper towels
- 2" foam brush
- Clear acrylic finish
- * Used in this project: DecoArt Americana Acrylic Paint, StenSource Stencils: 14" Round BD5703, 7" Garden Friends 2 BD9008, 3" Ivy Vine Border W7047

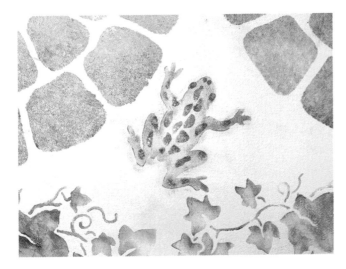

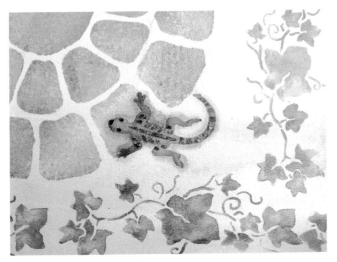

1 Paint the floorcloth with a base coat of light parchment using the mini foam roller and the paint tray.

2 Pour small amounts of caramel, raw umber and light parchment paint onto a paper or plastic plate. Use a dampened sea sponge to randomly sponge colors onto the stepping stone stencil. Mix colors on the stone areas. Remove the stencil and allow to dry. The stencils are placed next to each other with two motifs on the floorcloth.

3 Stencil the ivy using celery green paint. Highlight it with the the avocado paint.

4 Stencil the lizard on the stone using caramel paint. Highlight the body center with celery green. Use raw umber and black for the spots.

5 Stencil the second lizard using neutral grey paint. Highlight the body center with wash white. Use caramel and black for the spots.

6 Stencil the frog using raw umber paint. Highlight the body center with wash white. Use a combination of black and neutral grey for the spots.

7 Seal the floorcloth with one to two coats of clear acrylic finish using a foam brush.

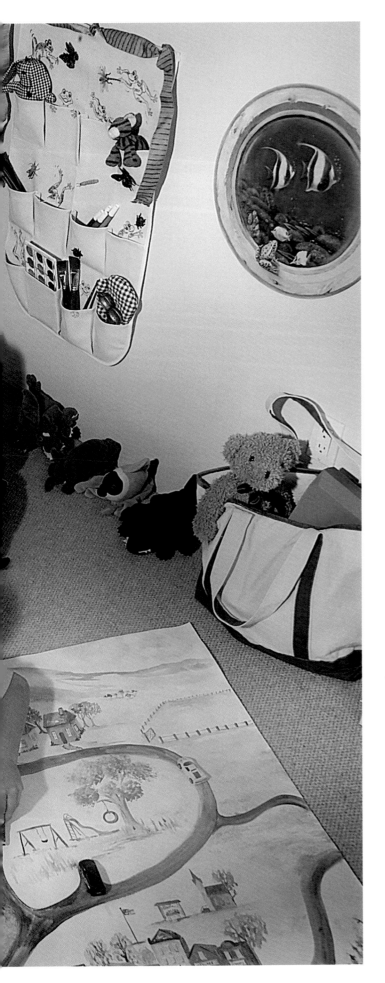

Chapter ⑦

Child's **Play**

How often do you hear the phrase "I'm bored" from your kids? I came up with a way to make sure they'll *have fun* and help their imagination grow. The unusual leap-frog twist on an old favorite is the Rolled Canvas Checkerboard. Instead of black and red checkers, I've used a frog theme on the game pieces.

Kids can keep this and other toys, like the Canvas Beanbags, in the handy Hanging Pocket Game Holder. This is also a great project to get the kids involved with, as well. Let them decide where to stencil the jumping frogs. While they're painting, protect their clothes with the Painter's Apron. You'll be glad you did.

The most ambitious project in this chapter is the Interactive Floorcloth. Kids will challenge their imaginations and have fun spending hours playing. The patterns are included, but you can customize the floorcloth to look like your home town. You can also *share memories* with the kids by encouraging their participation in making the Family Photo Album Cover. You won't have to wait for a rainy day to start having fun.

Hanging Pocket **Game Holder**

I'm sort of partial to *frogs*. You see, my uncle, Lee Giudici, is in the Guinness Book of World Records for the longest frog jump at the Calaverous County Frog Jump in Angels Camp, California. Actually, it is Lee's frog, "Rosie the Ribiter," who holds the record at 21 feet, 5¾" in 1986. I'm proud to say that I'm a part of the team, along with my husband, daughter and two grandchildren. When Lee's wife, Henrietta, was asked once how she makes the frog jump, her simple reply was, "you just go out on the stage, act like a fool, and the frog does the rest." There's just something *irresistible* about frogs that brings out the kid in all of us.

Materials

- Purchased canvas pocket panel (mine had three rows of four pockets)
- Fabric markers, tropical colors*
- Black permanent marker, extra fine line*
- Transfer paper in a color (red, for example)
- Frog patterns (see page 134)
- Pencil

- Heavy-duty tacky glue
- Bag of plastic bugs
- 2 yd. decorative ribbon (1½" wide)
- * Used in this project: Yasutomo Fabric Mate Markers, Yasutomo Black Permanent Extra Fine Line Marker, Crafter's Pick "The Ultimate"

Designer **Secrets**

Children especially get a kick out of the frog placement on this pocket game holder. But if they are too small to tackle drawing on the project, purchase an inexpensive white t-shirt that they can enjoy working on beside you.

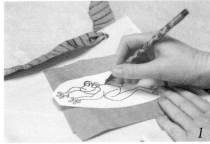

1 Using the frog pattern, trace the frogs onto the front of a canvas pocket using a pencil and the colored transfer paper.

2 Place the frogs as if they are jumping in and out of the pockets. Use the frog leg pattern where you want the frogs jumping into the pockets. Refer to the finished project for placement.

3 Outline the frogs in dark green using the fabric markers.

4 Color in the frogs with lime, yellow and green fabric markers. Blending colors with the fabric markers is easy and fun, too. Make some of the spots on the frogs green and orange.

5 Outline the frog's eyes with green and color them in with blue. Add details with the extra fine line black permanent marker.

6 Place the plastic bugs randomly over the pockets and adhere them to the canvas with heavy-duty tacky glue. Let dry flat.

7 Weave the decorative ribbon through the grommet holes on top of the pocket panel. Fill the pockets with paints, paintbrushes, soft stuffed animals, games and other fun stuff.

Rolled Canvas **Checkerboard**

I found that while the game of checkers can certainly be a lot of *fun*, it seems to be more fun when the checkers are turtles and butterflies and the checkerboard is metal green and blue. Monica and Cody were supposed to be taking a break during the photo shoot, but Craig, my photographer, found them playing checkers at the table—the children's spontaneity made a *wonderful* real-time photo.

The checkerboard can be rolled and placed inside an empty plastic wrap or aluminum foil tube. Because the canvas is double primed, it flattens out easily and quickly and the paint does not crack. The checkers can be stored in a zip closure bag inside the tube, as well.

Materials

- 13" x 13" double primed canvas
- No-prep metal paint*: 2 oz. each bright blue and bright lime green
- 1" foam brush
- Flat artist brush (1" wide)
- Mini foam roller
- Painter's blue tape (1" wide)
- Ruler
- Pencil
- Blue permanent marker, medium point
- 26 flat round wood discs (1" diameter)
- Woodburner with butterfly and turtle branding tips*
- Watercolor pencils*: true blue, lilac and spring green
- Spray shellac or 2 oz. acrylic satin finish
- Scissors
- * Used in this project: DecoArt No-Prep Metal Paint, Wall Lenk Woodburner, Prismacolor Watercolor Pencils

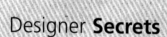

Designer **Secrets**

I was amazed to see that when I used the metal paint on the canvas, I was left with a finish that looked as though I had clear-coated the canvas with a durable and washable finish. Think outside the painter's box; metal paint is not just for metal.

1 Use a foam brush or mini foam roller to paint the 13" x 13" canvas front and back with bright lime green metal paint. Let one side dry before painting the opposite side.

2 Measure in 2½" all around the canvas square to make an 8" x 8" box in the center of the canvas.

3 Divide the inside square into 1" squares, eight across and eight down. Measure and mark them with a pencil.

4 If needed, tape off the squares using painter's blue tape to keep a clean crisp edge when painting the 1" alternating squares with bright blue. Paint every other square with bright blue metal paint using the 1" foam brush. Allow to dry.

5 Use a ruler and medium point blue permanent marker to outline the outside of the checkerboard.

Checkers

1 Attach the butterfly branding tip to the woodburning tool. Plug it in and follow the manufacturer's instructions for use. Brand half of the wood discs with the butterfly branding tip.

2 Use pliers to remove the hot butterfly branding tip. Do not touch the hot tool! Attach the turtle tip with pliers (another option is to unplug the tool, let it cool, and then change tips). Brand the other half of the wood discs with the turtle design.

3 Use the watercolor pencils to color in the branded butterfly and turtle designs as you desire.

4 Spray the finished checkers with shellac or brush them with a thin coat of acrylic satin finish.

Canvas **Beanbags**

Beanbags have been *tossed* for decades. There are many versions of the game's origin, but one thing I know for sure is that if you give people a bean bag, they will toss it. These beanbags are easy to stitch up and make great traveling companions for little ones to get out of a car and toss around. They are also the perfect entertainment to keep in the toy box when children visit.

You can even incorporate these into the other projects for *fun games*. Make up a "toss-the-frog" game with the interactive floorcloth by trying to toss the beanbags into the pond. Or draw some chalk lily pads on the sidewalk and see how close the beanbags get. It's all part of the fun in this age-old game.

Materials

- Instructions and materials are for 1 bean bag. Adjust as necessary for more.
- 2 squares of 6" x 6" unprimed canvas
- Small sandwich-size zip closure bag
- Bag of uncooked barley
- Frog patterns (see page 134)
- Fabric markers, tropical colors*
- Transfer paper in a color (red, for example)
- Pencil
- * Used in this project: Yasutomo Fabric Mate Markers

Designer Secrets

- I found it necessary to zigzag stitch around the bean bag twice to be sure the bag was securely closed and also to keep the cut edges from fraying.
- To remove as much of the air as possible from the zip closure bag, seal the closure almost all the way, insert a drinking straw into the opening and suck out the air. Quickly remove the straw and seal the closure the rest of the way.

1 Place the jumping frog pattern on the front of one 6" square of canvas. Trace around the pattern using transfer paper and a pencil.

Color in orange spots.

Color in purple eyes.

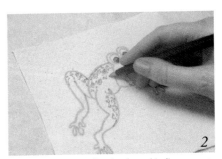

Color the frog skin lime green.

2 Outline the frog in the dark green fabric marker. Color the frog in the same manner as on the Pocket Game Holder (see page 110).

3 Place the front square and the other 6" square wrong sides together. Machine zigzag on a tight setting around all four sides, leaving a 4" opening on one side.

4 Place a zip closure sandwich bag inside of the beanbag. Pour in about ½- ¾ cup barley. Squeeze out the air in the bag and seal tightly. Stuff the rest of the barley-filled zip closure bag into the beanbag completely and continue to machine zigzag to close the opening.

Painter's **Apron**

There was definitely fun involved on my part as I was creating this painting apron project—spraying here and spritzing there. The project went *so fast* that I wanted to create one for each family member. When Monica put on the painter's apron and picked up the artist's brush, the *personality* of the little artist and the painter's apron combined into a big smile. I knew that the fun was in the creating and the giving.

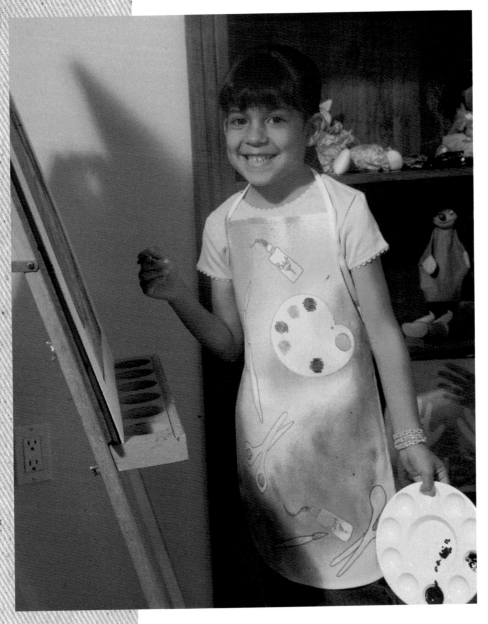

Materials

- Child-sized canvas apron
- Color spray*: lime green, crimson red, lemon peel and grape
- Fabric markers, standard colors*
- Heavy-duty poster board or thin cardboard
- Child's scissors, paint brushes, palette and paint tube patterns (see page 138)

- Paper towels
- Scissors
- Iron
- Plastic trash bag
* Used in this project: Duncan Tulip Cool Color Spray, Yasutomo Fabric Mate Markers

1 Press out any creases in the apron.

2 Cut open a plastic trash bag and cover the work surface to protect it from the spray paint. Place the apron on the covered work surface.

3 Trace the child's scissors, paint brushes, palette and paint tube onto the poster board or cardboard. Cut out the patterns.

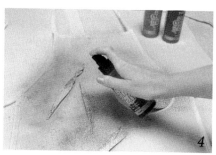

4 Place the pattern pieces on the apron. Randomly spray over them with the color spray, overlapping the colors.

Designer **Secrets**

This is a great project to create with a group of children. Think about using other objects as patterns. Gather leaves and flowers on a field trip or use bits of trims, string, lace, buttons and other found objects to spray around and over.

5 Lift up the pattern pieces and place them onto paper towels. Let the apron dry.

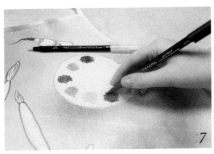

7 Squiggle with each fabric marker on the palette pattern on the apron to look like paint.

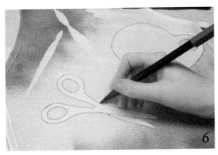

6 Outline the patterns on the apron with blue, green and purple fabric markers.

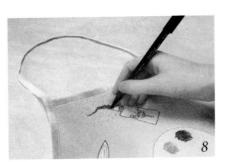

8 Write the word Paint on the paint tube.

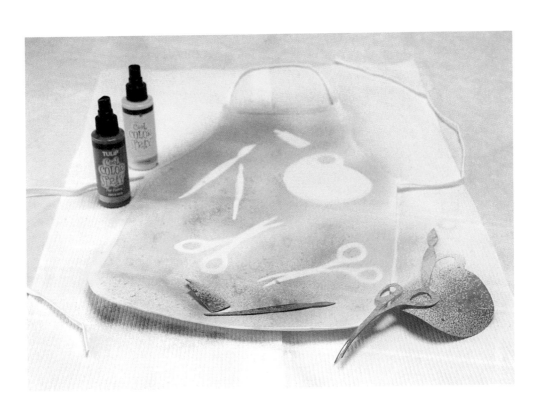

Interactive **Floorcloth**

Adapt this floorcloth to your own home town, adding any details that *personalize* the area. For example, paint the names on the buildings similar to those you may have in your home town. Paint the house the color of your home. As you can see from the smiles on the children's faces, a simple piece of floorcoth and a little paint will bring *hours of fun* for years to come.

Materials

- 4 foot x 6 foot double primed canvas
- Interactive floorcloth patterns (see pages 141-143)
- Flat artist brush (1½" wide)
- Angled flat brush (½" wide)
- #6 round artist brush
- #8 round artist brush
- Liner artist brush
- 2" foam brush
- 1½" foam brush
- Pencil
- Transfer paper
- Paper or plastic plate
- Natural sea sponge
- Acrylic paint*: 2 oz. each burnt umber, wash white, avocado, light avocado, black forest green, yellow green, primary blue, bright yellow, tomato red, traditional burnt umber, dioxazine purple and ultramarine blue
- Water container
- Paper towels

* Used in this project: DecoArt Americana Acrylic Paints

1 Refer to the finished photo of the floorcloth for the placement of the buildings, trees, pond, etc. (see page 125). Use the transfer paper and pencil to trace the patterns onto the floorcloth.

2 Pour some of each paint color onto a paper or plastic plate.

3 Draw a road with a pencil and use a 1½" wide foam brush to paint the road traditional burnt umber. Highlight the road with wash white using a 2" wide foam brush.

(see page 125)

4

4 Draw an irregular circle shape approximately 24" in diameter on the right side of the floorcloth. Poor some ultramarine blue on a paper or plastic plate. Paint the pond this color using the 2" foam brush. Make a thin wash of yellow green paint mixing ⅔ paint to ⅓ water. Use the 1½" wide flat artist brush to paint diagonal brush strokes across the rest of the canvas to the right of the houses.

5

5 While the wash is wet, use a dampened sea sponge and dab over the painted surface, which will soften the wash.

Designer **Secrets**

• No two floorcloths will look the same because paint and water, or washes, aren't absorbed into the canvas the same way twice. If I were to paint this floorcloth again, it would probably look completely different, even following the same design layout.

• The basic painting techniques can be applied to the entire floorcloth. The painting technique on the house is the same for the buildings, just change the colors and add the details you wish.

• Paint washes are simply water mixed with a little acrylic paint. The more paint, the more opaque the wash; the less paint, the more translucent the wash.

• DecoArt makes a product called Brush 'n Blend Extender, which is a water-based medium, that, when mixed with acrylic paint, extends the drying and blending times.

6

6 To paint the tree trunk and branches, make a wash of traditional burnt umber and water using ⅔ traditional burnt umber to ⅓ water. Using the flat angled artist brush, paint the base of the trunk about 2" wide. As you move up the tree trunk, paint some branches by turning the angled brush up on its edge to gradually taper each branch smaller as the branches extend out from the tree trunk. Use the #6 small round artist brush to paint smaller branches extending off the main tree branches. To make tree foliage, dip a sea sponge into avocado paint and lightly sponge over and around the branches. Turn your wrist to the left or right as you sponge the next foliage so that the sponge pattern is different over the entire tree.

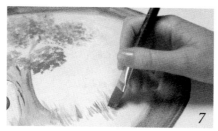

7 Dip the tips of the ½" angled flat artist brush into avocado paint and brush on wispy foliage blades.

8 Paint lilacs by dipping the tips of the #6 small round brush into dioxazine purple and painting small dots on the foliage.

9 Clean the brush and repeat the process in Step 7, but paint small dots of wash white over the foliage. The lilacs do not need to be dry to complete this step.

10 Mix some wash white and primary blue together on a paper or plastic plate. Paint a wash on the front and side of the house using the ½" angled artist brush.

11 Increase the amount of primary blue to the wash and paint a shadow under the roof and down the side of the house using the same ½" angled artist brush.

12 Paint the chimney with a wash of tomato red using the #6 small round artist brush.

13 Paint the windows bright yellow using the #6 small round artist brush.

14 Paint the roof with a wash of traditional burnt umber using the ½" angled artist brush.

15 Use the #6 small artist brush dipped in tomato red to paint around the windows, paint the front door and add details to the roof.

16 Use the #6 small round artist brush dipped in a wash of traditional burnt umber to paint the tree trunks and branches.

17 Use the #6 small round artist brush dipped into a wash of light avocado to dab on more tree foliage. While the paint is wet, dab on a wash of black forest green. The two colors will softly blend.

18 Dip the tips of the ½" angled flat brush into black forest green paint and stipple the paint on a slight d iagonal slope to the tree trunk, just the way the branches grow naturally.

19 Use the #6 small round artist brush to paint the pine tree trunk.

20 Use the liner artist brush dipped in wash white to paint waves on the pond.

21 Use the ½" wide artist brush dipped in a wash of yellow green to paint the field of green above the pond. The wash is a 50/50 mixture of paint and water. Drag the brush down the field. Leave some white areas and overlap the wash to add some darker areas.

22 Dip the ½" flat artist brush into water and then into a little ultramarine blue paint. Paint the sky, dipping the brush into the paint or water as needed to blend the color across the canvas.

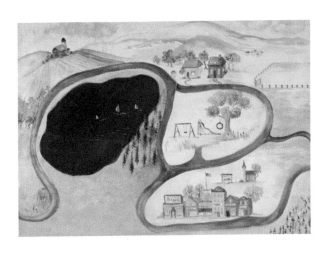

Family Photo
Album Cover

Children grow up so quickly. They bring us *treasures* from school of handmade plaster casts with their handprint and name marked in it. Or they manage to sneak a hand stamp in wet concrete! Using their handprints on family albums is a great way to keep up with the years of their lives and a *wonderful* way to label the albums as they grow.

Materials

- Purchased fabric photo album, white, if possible
- Color spray*: lemon peel and hot pink
- Fabric markers, standard colors*
- Poster board or thin cardboard
- Plastic trash bag
- Wax paper
- Paper towels
- Scissors
- * Used in this project: Duncan Tulip Cool Color Spray, Yasutomo Fabric Mate Markers

Designer Secrets

Have the children sign their own names and ages on their hands.

1 Cut a plastic trash bag open and cover the work surface to protect it from the color spray. Place the photo album on the covered work surface. Protect the inside of the photo album with wax paper.

2 Trace a child's handprint on the poster board or cardboard or use your own handprint, adjusting the size of the drawing to make it smaller.

3 Cut out at least four total handprints. Reverse the patterns for left and right handprints.

4 Place them on the front of the photo album.

5 Lightly mist around the hands with the lemon peel color spray.

6 Lift up the handprints and reposition them on the photo album, overlapping some of the first handprints.

7 Lightly mist around the hands with hot pink color spray.

8 Place the handprint cut-outs on paper towels. Lightly spray the cut-outs with hot pink and place them face-down onto the photo album. Lightly press to create a positive design. Do not overspray or the cut-out will drip.

9 Remove the cut-outs and allow the photo album to dry.

10 Add the child's name and age with fabric markers.

About the Author

Bunny's grandmother was the first to recognize her talents as she watched her 7-year-old granddaughter design clothes for her Barbie doll. Her natural abilities led to a long career in home arts and interior design. Bunny has worked with more than a hundred manufacturers designing, developing and demonstrating products. Her creative projects have been published in dozens of booklets and magazines.

Over the past ten years, Bunny has appeared on numerous television programs sharing her innovative projects with thousands of viewers. She co-hosted her own program, "Your Home Studio," bringing her home décor expertise to the popular TNN network. Bunny's practical experience and innate talent has been a contributor to her success as a class instructor as well.

In 1991, Bunny created Fe Fi Faux Finish®, a professional faux finishing and decorative painting business. She has also invented and designed Trompe L'Oeil Wall Décor™, a line of pre-pasted wall murals as well as accessories for the home and garden.

Bunny's latest business venture, Homes Dressed To Sell®, combines her love of home décor with the excitement of the real estate market. She optimizes the interiors of hard-to-sell homes by rearranging existing furnishings or bringing furniture and accessories into vacant homes. As a result, homes that have been on the market for many months usually sell within a short period of time. Bunny is also a professional realtor.

This is Bunny's first book, and she has created a formula for identifying stylish yet easy-to-make home décor projects, all from canvas.

Bunny can be reached on the Web at www.fefifaux.com or www.homesdressedtosell.com.

Resources

Canvas Concepts
1415 Bancroft Ave.
San Francisco, CA 94124
http://www.canvasconcepts.com
Primed canvas, double primed canvas, canvas fabric, canvas panels and floorcloths.

Cook's Photography
2301 Skyway Drive Suite D
Santa Maria, CA 93455
(805) 614-9440
http://www.cooksdigital.com
Printed canvas (printed images of Interactive Floorcloth, Patio Floorcloth and Veggie Prints)

Crafter's Pick™
Adhesive Products Inc. (API) Crafter's Pick, Albany, CA
http://www.crafterspick.com
Glues: The Ultimate and Memory Mount
Finishes: Craqueleur

Craftware
Four Oaks, NC
http://www.craft-ware.com
Red liner tape: various widths, lengths and shapes

DecoArt™
Attn: Craft Division
PO Box 327
Stanford, KY 40484
http://www.decoart.com
Americana™ Acrylic Paints, Patio Paint™, No-Prep™ Metal Paint, Brush 'n Blend™ Extender and Faux Glazing Medium™

Duncan Enterprises
5673 East Shields Ave.
Fresno, CA 93727
http://www.duncancrafts.com
Tulip® Cool Color Spray™, Soft™ Brushable Fabric Paint and Rub-On Transfers™, Aleene's® Platinum Bond™ Super Fabric Textile Adhesive

Krylon®
http://www.krylon.com
18K Gold Leafing Pen and Copper Leafing Pen

Plaid® Enterprises
Attn: Customer Service
PO Box 2835
Norcross, GA 30091-2835
http://www.plaidonline.com
FolkArt® Acrylic Paint and Brush Cleaner & Conditioner

StenSource® International
18971 Hess Ave.
Sonora, CA 95379
http://www.stensource.com
Stencils and stencil brushes

Wall Lenk Corporation
PO Box 3349
Kinston, NC 28501
(888) 527-4186
http://www.wlenk.com
Electric Stencil Cutting Pen, Transfer Tool, woodburning tool and decorative branding tips

Yasutomo & Co.
South San Francisco, CA
http://www.yasutomo.com
Fabric Mate™ Fabric Marking Pens and PermaWrite Pens

Veggie and Fruit Designs
Shown at 100%

Zebra Pattern
Shown at 100%

Frog Patterns
Shown at 100%

Crocodile Pattern
Enlarge 118%

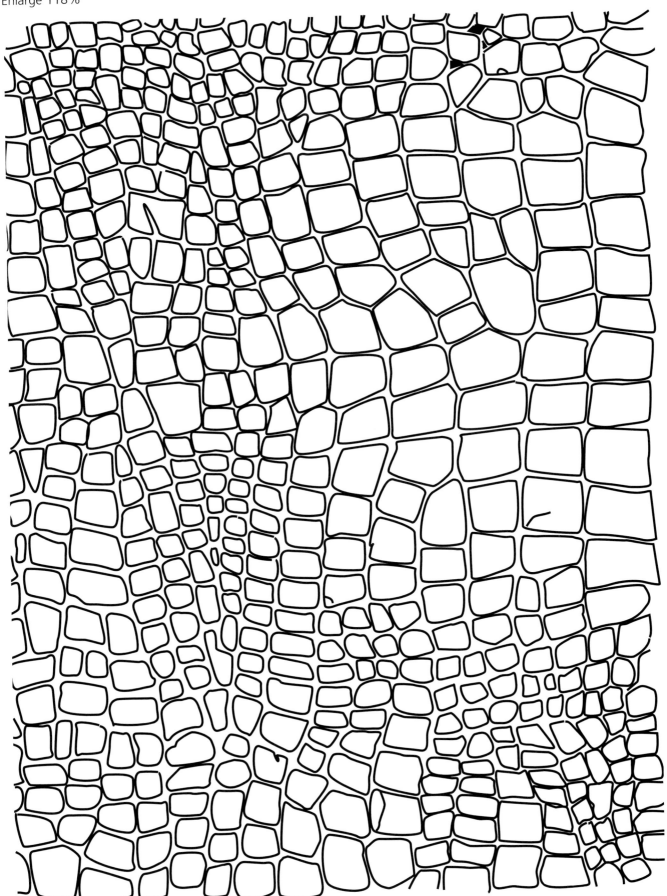

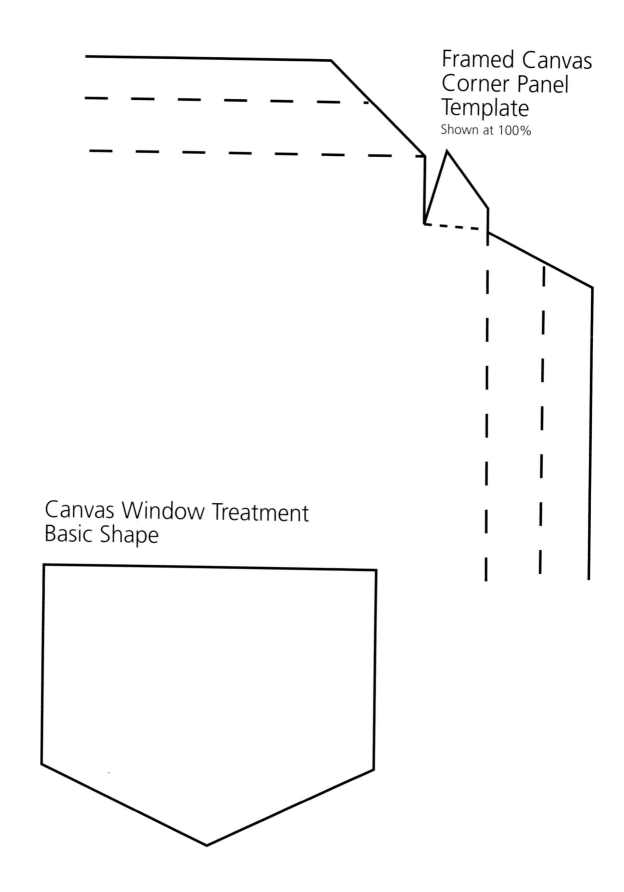

Framed Canvas
Corner Panel
Template
Shown at 100%

Canvas Window Treatment
Basic Shape

Trapezoid Pattern
Shown at 100%

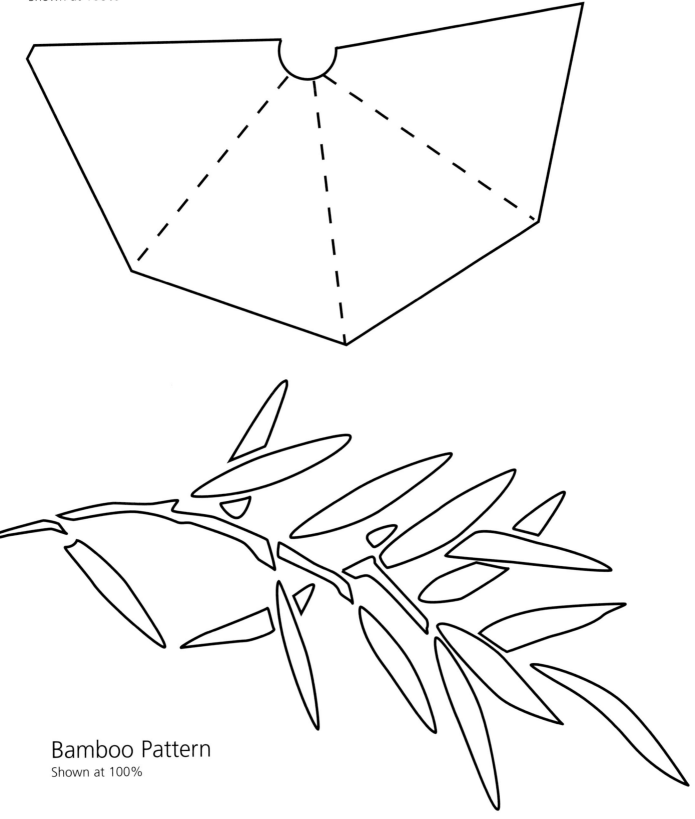

Bamboo Pattern
Shown at 100%

Child's Scissors, Paint Brushes, Palette and Paint Tube Patterns

Shown at 100%

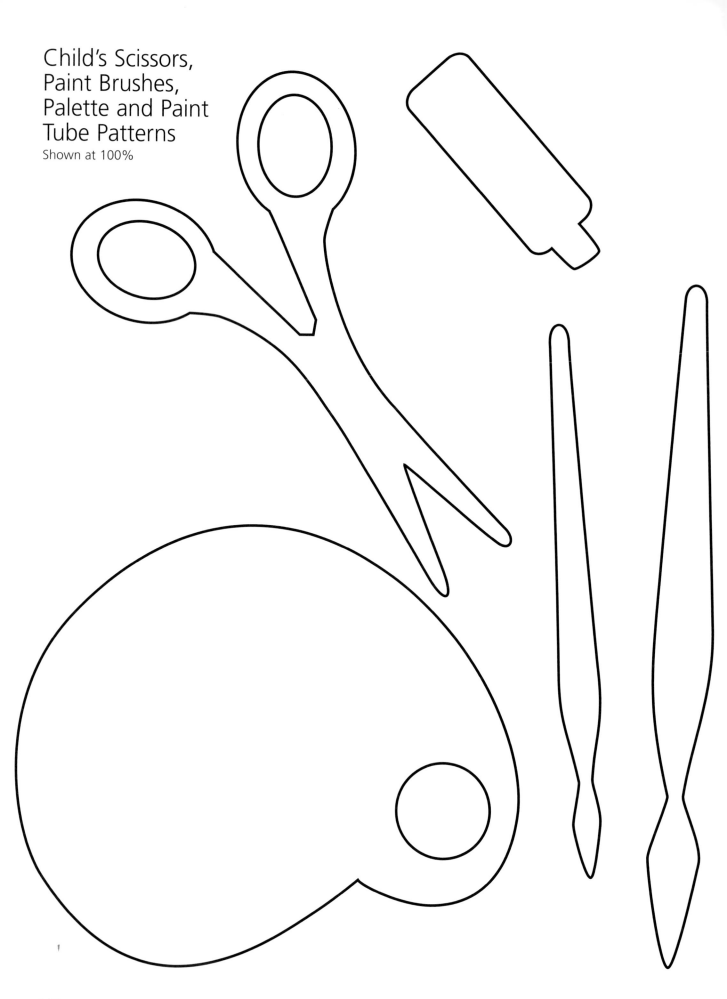

Palm Tree Pattern
Shown at 100%

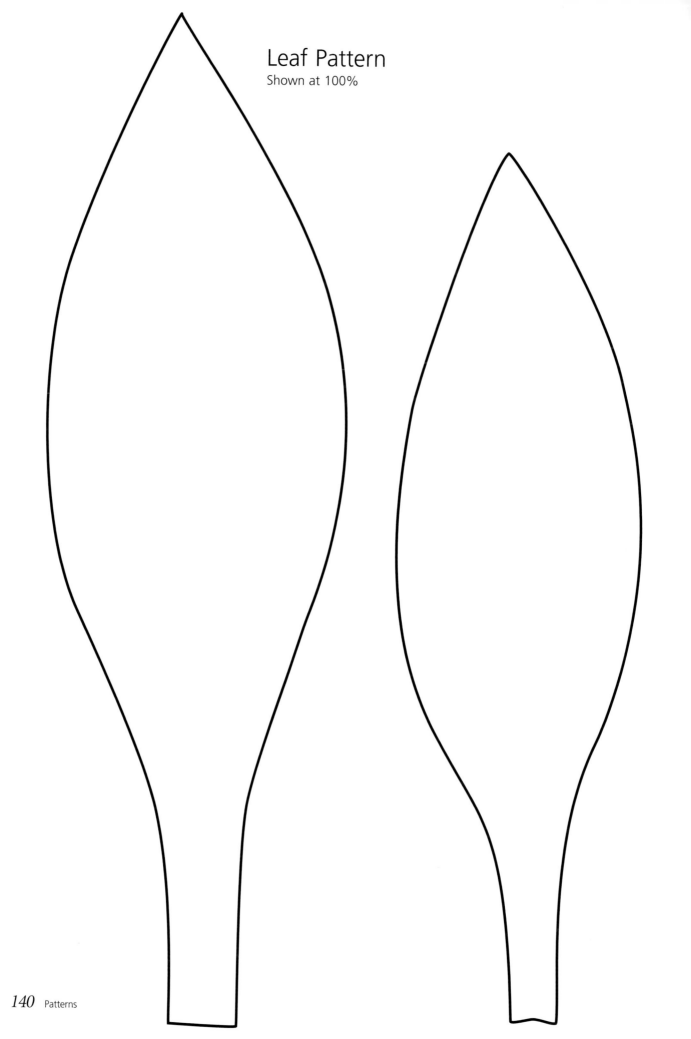

Leaf Pattern
Shown at 100%

Interactive Floorcloth Patterns

Shown at 100%

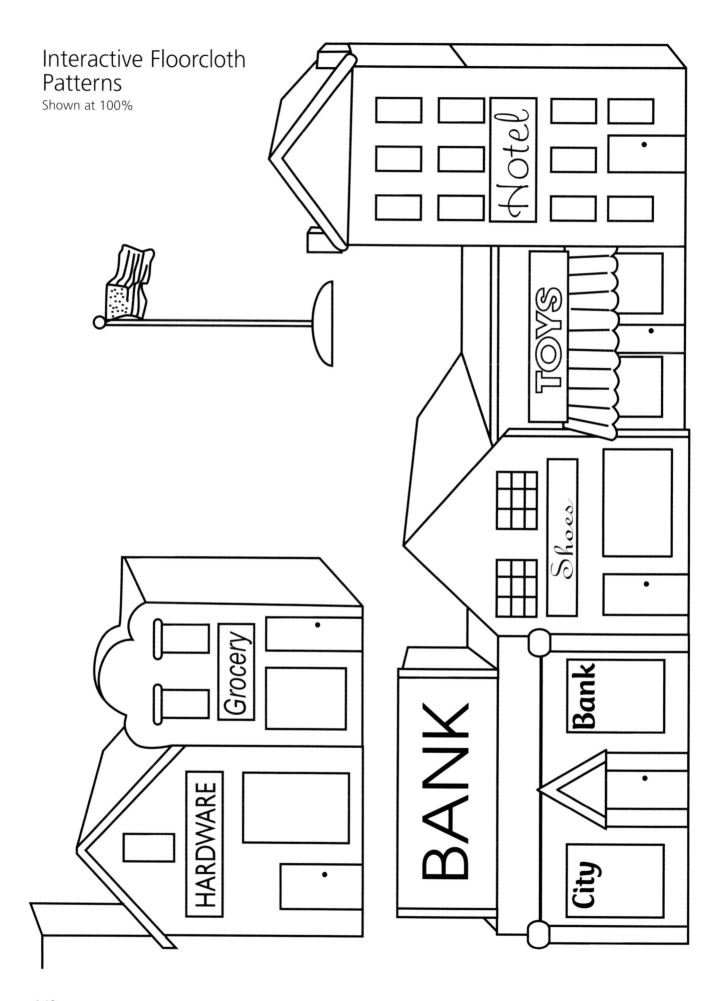

Interactive Floorcloth
Patterns
Shown at 100%

Tropical Leaf Pattern
Shown at 100%